CATFISH DREAM

Southern Foodways Alliance

Studies in Culture, People, and Place

The series explores key themes and tensions in food studies—
including race, class, gender, power, and the environment—on a
macroscale and also through the microstories of men and women
who grow, prepare, and serve food. It presents a variety of voices,
from scholars to journalists to writers of creative nonfiction.

Series Editor
John T. Edge

CATFISH DREAM

ED SCOTT'S FIGHT FOR HIS FAMILY FARM AND RACIAL JUSTICE IN THE MISSISSIPPI DELTA

JULIAN RANKIN

THE UNIVERSITY OF GEORGIA PRESS   ATHENS

A Sarah Mills Hodge Fund Publication

This publication is made possible in part through a grant
from the Hodge Foundation in memory of its founder,
Sarah Mills Hodge, who devoted her life to the relief and
education of African Americans in Savannah, Georgia.

Library of Congress Control Number: 2018937821
ISBN: 9780820353609 (hardback)
ISBN: 9780820353593 (paperback)
ISBN: 9780820353616 (e-book)

For Caroline and little Julian, for the Scotts,

and for families everywhere who endure, tell stories, and

give their children the gifts of legacy and namesake

The catfish didn't miss the current. They'd never known it. They lapped the pond all day like pace cars. At feeding time, they thrashed for their share of pellets. The farmers bred them for size and taste and texture and profit. They swam around in that little man-made lake and waited for the chopping block and the flash-frozen package. Their bodies were bullion. There were others of them, wild ones, who lived in the open waters of the river to the west. They sometimes got caught on the trotlines of grizzled river rats. Mostly they grew big as they pleased and swam deep into the crevices of the underwater earth. Fishermen told stories. "He had whiskers big as bullwhips." Men saw fleeting visions of this barnacled ghost ship. If you caught him and ate him, they said, you'd gain all the wisdom of a century. He was part whale. Too big for the line. You could tell it was he by the waves he made when he breached the surface.

CONTENTS

PART II. STALK

PART III. REAP

INTRODUCTION

Babe Ruth wasn't born a sultan (of swat) or a king (of swing). He grew up an unruly and unsupervised Baltimore youth, and a Catholic brother named Matthias molded him into rawhide-slugging form. I learned this in first grade. Before, I had been certain that all people who did great things had always been great. But George Washington the man wasn't carved out of marble. There was a time when he didn't tower over folks, when his hairdo wasn't powdered, when he was one of us.

In Mississippi Delta history, farmer Edward Logan Scott Jr. is legend. During his lifetime, many thought of him as mythic; others, pure myth. I sat with him for hours of sprawling conversation. From his wheelchair in a dimly lit living room he recounted his history. The Scott family opened their archives to me and shared the story of Scott's father, Edward Sr., who brought the family to Mississippi in the 1920s. Edward Sr. left his job in Alabama as a postman and farmer to find more prosperous conditions. Ed Scott Jr., born in 1922, lived into his father's pioneering history and built upon it. When he dug up 160 acres of arable farmland and turned them into catfish ponds in 1981, gossip and folktale made it sound like black magic. If it is magic, it can't be duplicated. But if exceptionalism is man-made, then it can be made again.

I learned to write a book by writing this book. When I hit roadblocks, I looked to my interviews with Scott for guidance. I applied his philosophies about catfish and activism. The first draft was digging the ponds. And then stocking. And feeding. And so on. The intimidating scope of a first book—line after line, page after page, season after season—encompassed infinite fields of rice and beans too giant to conceptualize until, one pass at a time up and down the furrows like a farmer, it wasn't any longer. I came to see my own brief Mississippi Delta childhood in concert with Scott's story. I was a toddler playing down by the cotton gin in Shaw in 1989 when Scott was a half hour away in Leflore County battling the government to keep his farm afloat.

When I lived in the Delta as a boy, every little thing that happened had shades of life and death, and nothing that happened in the wider world shook my immediate existence. I trusted only what was in my vision or grasp. I loved a cat named Rupert, who roamed at night on the hunt for mice across the street at the old cotton gin. One day we found Rupert dead in the driveway. My mother put him in a black garbage bag, and we buried him in the yard below a little molehill two feet high. My mother told me it was the highest point in the Delta, and I believed her.

Stories like Ed Scott's are not only Mississippi and southern tales, but American ones. Their characters contend with both human and nature, from the prejudice of their neighbors and the collateral consequences of political ambitions to failing infrastructure and the wrath of the drought and flood. When most of his peers farmed 40-, 80-, or 120-acre plots, Scott farmed thousands. He had the entrepreneurial savvy of a railroad baron. To borrow from a well-known contemporary poet, put Scott anywhere on God's green earth and he'd triple his worth. His accomplishments flowed out to and benefitted others, primarily the surrounding Delta communities of black farmers and families. In its totality, Scott's life serves up questions about who we ought to be—as a collective nation in service to our diversity of citizens, and as citizens striving for our perfect parcel of the American dream.

I knew Ed Scott for only a short time. I do not know his every secret. But when he unfurled his story before me, it had his soul in it. I met Scott in his dwindling sunset. I followed him backward through time. Layers of the man, the soldier, the boy. Not just old. Not only young. Scott the ageless—a man for all ages. A man who should be remembered.

PART I SEED

1 FAMILY LAND

An American flag, sun-bleached, hung motionless from its pole on the front of the farmhouse. The air was humid. Thick like paraffin. The sky was clear, but Ed Scott Jr., seated behind an aluminum desk in his office, sensed gathering clouds. More thunder. And fire.

He reclined in a wooden chair, in a button-up shirt that read "Scott's Fresh Catfish" tucked into jeans. Scott's eyes darted. He inspected the familiar room and reviewed a mental checklist. Invoices peeped out of folders. More dust floated in the air, caught in the light, than he would prefer. Things needed doing. His belly hung slightly over his belt. He was a well-fed sixty-seven. He wore a farm cap on his head, and a mustache bristled above his upper lip. It was 1989.

Scott had bought the desk and the filing cabinets and everything else from an industrial office supply manufacturer. Thousands of other offices in a hundred other American industries probably had the same functional suite. Everything but the chair. Scott had been more particular about his swiveling desk chair. It needed a cushion, stature, and durability. Like Red Wing boots or a John Deere Model A tractor, whose own captain's seat Scott considered the paragon. Things of quality like the chair need only be acquired once, Scott believed. They should last forever. Like family land.

The building in which Scott sat was a catfish-processing plant built in the remote open fields of Leflore County. Scott began with an emaciated tractor shed built by his father and fleshed out his catfish headquarters atop the bones with poured concrete, cinder blocks, and stainless steel hardware. When he first got into catfish he didn't plan on having a processing plant. But Scott would become the first of his kind: the first

African American to dig and stock his own catfish ponds and vertically integrate his business. It was a move forced by the discriminatory practices of agents of the U.S. government. It was a move that exposed the very core of the establishment's bias.

Two ladies working with the Sunflower County Public Library in nearby Indianola sat across the table from Scott.[1] One, the interviewer, took notes. The other juggled a camera rig. Scott had cut his errands short to meet them here. He drove fast on the way over. He was a fast driver. Once, Scott said, a state trooper pulled him over for speeding and fined him a hundred dollars. "Let me go ahead and give you two hundred dollars now because I'm coming back the same way."[2]

The women thanked Scott for sitting with them. Scott answered that he didn't mind. He had been looking forward to telling his story.

How did the Scott family wrestle control of all this land when so many of their peers struggled as tenants? the ladies wanted to know. Why weren't there more like him?

In the Mississippi Delta, power is a stand-in for morality. The aldermen and commissioners and judges and cops and football coaches and landlords seem installed not by vote or appointment, but by on-high decree. They own the place. Here, what is rendered unto Caesar and rendered unto God go to the same P.O. box. Here, it's hard to get it if you don't already have it.

"Row crop farming was done in the early ages," Scott began. "I started with my father and I give him and the Lord credit for everything I've done here."

Scott gave voice to his father, Edward Sr., a man too busy to put his story on the record. Edward Sr. moved his family from Alabama to Mississippi in 1919. He worked shares in Glendora, around twenty miles away from the site of the future catfish plant. He sharecropped for nine years before he saved up enough to buy his first piece of farmland. In 1929, just before the Depression hit, Edward Sr. bought a new car. He built a garage and parked the Chevrolet inside, out of view, so that no one would know he had it. Edward Sr. did not hide his success—he protected it. Scott and his father shared the same aspiration: an American empire, for as many as it could feed.

"I left and went to the service in 1942," said Scott, "and when I got out I bought this piece of land where I live now [from my father]. When he passed, the family owned 1,080 acres here. From sharecropper to landowner. We was the first people, in 1947, to start growing rice. And any change that came around in the farming industry, my father would change with it."

The woman with the camera shifted the rig on her shoulder. The interviewer smiled at Scott as he spoke and nodded attentively. Scott took them to the early 1980s when he broke into the lucrative catfish business. Row cropping—mainly cotton, soybeans, and corn—fell away as the undisputed Delta moneymaker. Farmers looked elsewhere for financial viability. They excavated their fields and made fishponds. The government doled out huge loans. The catfish rush was on.

"But I built the ponds out of my pocket," Scott added. No subsidy, his own equipment, and very little blueprint. He dug almost every day for a year. Eight ponds—160 endless acres of dirt—just outside the office window and across the dirt road from the house where Scott and his wife, Edna, slept.

To dig the ponds, three generations of Scott men relied on a variety of tractors and backhoes and machines and laser levels, including the Case, a brawny machine with big tread and a gritty engine that purred like a happy cat. By noonday sun and moonlight, the men carved out the grave-deep basins. They rattled behind the wheel for stretches of hours. The vibrations from the ride stayed with them after the day was done, a persistent internal hum that tingled the body.

The men dug in the spirit of the ancients, inverting the native people's mound-building history during the Mississippi Period before Europeans arrived. They had constructed spiritual gathering places and celestial crossroads; Scott tamped terrestrial mud to hold his modern business. A neighbor could have watched the ponds take shape from across the road in the live oak shade of the Scott family cemetery—nearly a dozen scattered, moss-worn stones with epitaphs in various states of legibility. Edward Sr., at rest here, looked on.

"My motto is don't stop chasing your dream," said Scott. "And that was my dream. To grow these catfish. Which I did. . . . If I could've got the money to keep them going, you could expect $468,000 a year, and to operate the ponds after they were up and running would cost you $250,000 a year. Now you see how much profit. That's why you get in the catfish business. Because it's a business."

Scott looked at the ladies, stuck on a thought. "Now let me tell you why I'm in this mess, which you really need to know."

2 CHASING THE DREAM

Scott had ponds. He needed fish. He applied for and received a loan of $150,000 from the Farmers Home Administration (FmHA), a subsidiary of the U.S. Department of Agriculture (USDA).

It wasn't enough to fund the operation, Scott said. "Just enough to get me in trouble."

It would take several hundred thousand dollars in the first year of the catfish operation to stock all the ponds with fingerlings, feed them out, and process them. Scott was able to stock only about half of his underwater acreage. He fed and raised the fish until they matured and were ready to go to market. Then he looked for somewhere to process them.

Delta Pride, a farmer-owned cooperative, processed more catfish than anybody. They'd opened a big plant 1981 in nearby Indianola and helped usher in the growing industry. But to process fish at Delta Pride, a farmer had to own stock in the company. When Scott tried to buy stock, he was denied. The reasoning, Scott recalled, was simple. He had the wrong color skin.

"Now you know what that did for me?" Scott said. "That said if the government was going to put money into something and I couldn't get no stock in it, the government was no better than the people in Mississippi."

Scott leaned forward and spoke softer. "You know, people used to think catfish was a salvage fish," he said, acknowledging the reputation of the bottom-feeding channel catfish. "Wouldn't nobody eat it. But now it's the gourmet of the line." Scott identified with underdogs.

With the door at Delta Pride closed to him, Scott built a facility of his own. When he opened his processing plant in 1983, it wasn't automated.

Workers hand-skinned until the company upgraded to band saws and stainless-steel tables and chutes and scales and conveyer belts. Hand-skinning was slower, but Scott and his crew could inspect and clean each fish thoroughly.

"Now everybody talks about how our fish tastes," Scott said. "We take pride in our fish. When we first started cleaning fish, we used to wash the inside out with a brush. Every one of them. We took all the black lining out . . . and it really tastes better.

"I didn't stop there. . . . We upgraded our plant in 1985 to what you see right now. Now we got seven skinners on the line, four head saws, got an eviscerator [to suck the guts out], everything that any other plant has. We have been inspected by USDC [U.S. Department of Commerce]. We can sell to anybody. . . . Right now we're hitting the shores of California. We're going to L.A. with it. Washington, Philadelphia, Chicago. We hope to go into vacuum packing and anything anybody else does in the next few months. Right now we have 34 full-time workers. We intend to expand our operation from 34 to 115."

Within a few years the plant would close. Even at the time of the video recording, those ponds across the way weren't full of fish. Scott was processing for other farmers and buying catfish—cash, a few at a time—to process and sell. The plan had been to stock the ponds and pond-hatch successive generations. But in 1983 the local FmHA office dubbed Scott's business a risky venture and refused to extend him further credit. The government took all the fish, their bodies still writhing and flopping. FmHA had a lien on them and decided to call it in. Banks—which actually made the government-secured distributions—foreclosed on roughly a thousand acres of Scott's farmland. The agency declined to restructure his loan or forgive his debt. Scott never farmed his own land again.

The ordeal began in 1978 when, after decades of farming, Scott heard that he could get this money from the government, which was pouring hundreds of millions into southern agriculture. Scott farmed with government money for a few short years. The decision proved costly. Whatever racial reconciliation had been realized since the middle 1960s wasn't evident in the government statistics, which told of USDA's continued disenfranchisement of black farmers. Scott's momentum waned—even if he wouldn't admit it to the interviewer in 1989. Every battle had been followed by another. After he lost his fish crop in 1983, he had no money left to restock. He bought fish from other farmers, Scott said, until FmHA issued veiled threats to those who sold fish to Scott. Scott held on to his ponds and his plant and his house. The rest he lost when the government foreclosed on him. The ponds would sit empty for the next thirty years. But the man persevered.

Scott took the ladies into the freezer room. The camera rolled. "Watch the floor, now. It's wet," Scott warned. "You cold?"

He pointed to a pallet jack stacked high. "You know where this is going?" Scott asked. The ladies didn't. It was going to Alcorn State University, the historically black college in rural Claiborne County, Mississippi. "Three thousand dollars' worth of fish going to Alcorn."

They exited through the loading dock and walked back into the sunlight. Birds chirped. Scott pointed to four long concrete vats, a few feet deep and wide, that could each hold thirty thousand pounds of live catfish. This is where the live haulers offloaded, where the fish got stunned with electricity before the workers sent them inside the plant to the head saws. Water dripped slowly out of a spigot—not quite shut off—into the empty vat. "When the fish get in there in the summer the flies tend to bother them. . . . We keep the fish in this trough with water running on top of them so the flies won't bother them at all."

The strips of woodland that cut through the Delta farmland are full of critters in the high grass and water moccasins in shallow ditches. This is still wild land. It was tamed and made arable in the preceding century, but the frontier seems always to be rapping at the door. In the woods, when an animal dies, nothing happens right away. There's no five-second rule. No one comes through to make sure the carcass meat makes it to the freezer. Carrion and scavengers and microbes don't mind. Eventually the thing will be gone, picked clean and decomposed. Capitalism doesn't give death such a wide berth. It mechanizes and feeds on it.

Scott believed the quality of his catfish depended on how quickly he could "chill him after you kill him." Death was only the beginning, a station along the journey from pond to skinning table to box in the Kroger freezer. Scott was generally impatient with nature's pace. He preferred direct action to passive voice, lucid vision to aimless dream. Henry Ford, Scott knew, had changed the world by harnessing man's engineering potential. Scott had a mind to do the same.

Before the crew left, the interviewer asked Scott what he would like to tell his great-great-grandchildren, knowing that the tape would be archived in the county library.

"Well if it's going in the library, I'd like to say to my people: It ain't no such thing as 'you can't do what you want to do' if you want to do it bad enough. If you put your hand and heart to anything you want to do, you can do it. . . . And you got to look at this. If you're on the bottom, what way is it to go but up?"

3   GOOD DIRT

Edward Scott Sr. was born in 1886 in Prairieville, Alabama, in Hale County. He'd been a postman there. He would wake up before the sun rose to deliver mail on mule-back. When he got through with his route in the evening, he'd come home to plow his field. He was a tall, stocky man with strong features. He gazed with certainty. He never cursed. He didn't drink; not unless it was really good moonshine. He'd laugh if you said something funny, but he didn't crack jokes.

Edward Sr. could read the land like his own palm. Riding atop the mule, plodding over the dirt every day, he came to know the earth's rhythm. One day he woke up early and went outside and saw his crop drowning—once again, as had happened before, flooded in the night. The fields shimmered. It was time to move on. It was time to go to Mississippi.

Edward Sr. headed west to scout for land. He found a man near Glendora, in the Mississippi Delta, for whom he could sharecrop. This boss man, remembered as Sell Jones, pointed Edward Sr. to his plot. Edward Sr. accepted the terms. He went home to Alabama and packed up his family. He sent them ahead on the train and rode in the freight car with the furnishings. After a few days in Mississippi, his wife, Juanita, wasn't happy. "We can't stay here," she pleaded. "These people are too mean. Send us back."[3]

Edward Sr. was resolute. "I believe I could stay in hell one year if I knew I could move out the next," he replied. That was that.

A midwife delivered Ed Scott Jr. on Sell Jones's plantation in 1922. He had no birth certificate. He was the seventh of ten surviving children. The second-to-last son. He joined older siblings Moses, Laighton, Samuel Winder, Alexander, Rosa Bell, and Susie B. Scott. Later came Mossouri Odessa, Harvey DeWitt, and Edna "Mae" Ruth.[4] All of them were raised in the fields.

Edward Sr. and his hardworking young children farmed so well that Sell Jones gave them more land to work. They had been farming for Sell Jones and making him money for two years when Edward Sr. started thinking about moving to Arkansas, where, it was rumored, land was available to black farmers. As Scott recalled the story, Sell Jones got wind of it and called Edward Sr. into his office in the general store away from the sharecropper houses. There, Sell Jones kept the ledger, tallied the debt, and meted out the sharecroppers' meager profits. Transactions happened through a hole in the glass.

"I've got to know one thing," Sell Jones said, offering him a seat. "Are you planning to move to Arkansas?"

"I thought about it," Edward Sr. said. "But I can't go now because I lost one of my horses."

"You lost one of your horses?!"

"I went to catch him and he snorted and ran backward and some barbed wire caught him and cut his back leg. And I took him down to the river and shot him because he was going to die."

"I sure hate to hear that," said Sell Jones, "because those were some pretty horses. Let me tell you what I'll do for you," he continued. "You don't go to Arkansas . . . Arkansas is too poor. Too unfriendly. They don't help you none there. Stay here another year with me. I'm going to give you all the crop you and the children can work. . . . Another thing I'm going to do. I'm going to settle with you just like I would settle with my brother. Now you take all that land I give you and work it, work it as long as you want to, make some money. [If you do that], I'll move you anywhere you want to go within twenty-five miles of here free of charge. Ain't going to charge you a nickel."

Sell Jones had motive for his paternalistic generosity. Edward Sr.'s boys were good workers. Sell Jones valued black labor and wanted to keep them. But he wouldn't, under any circumstance, entertain the idea of selling his land to black farmers.

After another year of successful farming, Edward Sr. took Sell Jones up on his offer. Edward Sr. found a place to rent a dozen or so miles away in a growing community of black farmers called Neukahoma. The roads to Edward Sr.'s new home were so bad that Sell Jones's men needed four mules to a wagon. The mule teams dragged the wagons through the mire, the wheels barely turning. They stopped in front of the house, and the drovers sat high and dry while Edward Sr. and his boys unloaded their things. Then Sell Jones's men, without a second look, turned around and went back. Edward Sr. never heard another word from Sell.

Edward Sr. farmed his rented land and worked as a farmhand for a white landowner, P. H. Brooks, managing five hundred acres for him. Brooks genuinely encouraged Edward Sr.'s ambition to be a landowner.

Around that time, Scott said, some land came up for sale in nearby Money, Mississippi. (Thirty years later, the tiny town of Money would be made infamous by the murder of Emmett Till.) When Edward Sr. showed up at the plantation storehouse in Money to introduce himself to the landowner, the man greeted him with a shotgun. "Get out of here, nigger! Get out of here before I blow your brains out!"

Edward Sr. left quickly. He went home worried, wondering what that man had against him. He went to some of his neighbors—who were also black farmers—and told them where he'd been. You should have told us you were headed over there, his neighbors said. Edward Sr. saw guilt in their eyes.

When the Money landowner had asked around about him, Edward Sr.'s neighbors replied that he was a good man. But also that he was out of his depth. That he thought he was white. Edward Sr. didn't think he was white. He believed he was equal.

Edward Sr. wasn't deterred. He soon found his land when P. H. Brooks parceled out and sold large portions of his property. He sold the east side to the black farmers and the west side to the whites. Edward Sr. was first in line to buy his piece. Brooks told Edward Sr. to pick his tract. He did.

A hundred acres right near the spot where the catfish plant would one day sit.

"I thought you'd go pick that place with running water," Brooks said to Edward Sr. There was already a house there and everything.

That was a good thing, Edward Sr. agreed. But a house and running water wouldn't make him any money. He needed land. And good dirt.

4 THE LITTLE GUY

Scott, from the time he could walk, shadowed his father and older brothers. When he was old enough—about seven—he slung an empty grain sack over his shoulder and went out in the field. His job was to fill the sack with a hundred pounds of cotton before the sun went down. His other job was to make sure the mules got water.

Little Scott could have climbed into the grain sack and slept, it was so big. The mules were big, too; they snorted at him and gave him looks that made him think they wanted to stomp him into mush. His father was big. His brothers were big. Their overalls were big. Scott wanted to be a giant. To step over the top of the cotton instead of trudging through the rows. He felt small. He clenched his little fists.

One morning, with the sun beating down, Scott took a break from picking cotton and came in from the fields to water the mules. He pumped their trough full. The thirsty mules shuffled over as one. Before Scott was a hundred yards away, they'd drained every drop.

Scott's older brother Laighton caught up with Scott as he walked away. "I told you to put water with the mules," he said.

"I did put water with the mules."

"There's none in the trough right now."

"I don't have nothing to do with that."

Laighton grabbed his younger brother by the collar and threw him to the ground, then hit him with a flurry of open hands. Scott curled up into a ball and braced himself. When he saw an opening, he grabbed Laighton's leg. He pulled it close and held on while Laighton kicked. Scott sank his teeth into the calf. He felt the skin give way.

"That's when I took a plug out," said Scott. "Just bit him through the pants."

That night, as he was nursing his gash, Laighton told his mother what had happened. She told Edward Sr., who called Scott into the bedroom. "Edward, what did you bite Laighton about?" he asked sternly.

Scott started crying. "Be—cause, he—was—whooping me," he gasped.

"Whooping you about what?"

"About those mules. I couldn't keep water," he cried.

Edward Sr. called Laighton. "What did you whoop Edward about?" he asked.

The empty trough, Laighton told him.

"Let me tell you one thing," Edward Sr. said to Laighton. "From now on, as long as he needs a whooping, you tell me. You're trying to make him pour water and pick cotton, and he can't do all that."

Scott wiped his eyes. He was still in his farm clothes. He went into the other room to change. Dishes clanged in the kitchen and his mother hummed a tune. He washed his hands so he'd be ready for dinner. The men piled their plates high. So did Scott. They ate deliberately. Scott took giant bites like his hungry brothers. He spooned in every drop of gravy. He felt the bruises purpling. His muscles ached. Laighton wore a bandage on his leg. They'd all been beaten by the day, by those undefeated laws of nature that laid, eventually, even powerful men low. But they were past that. The sun was down. Scott reached over the limas and grabbed another roll. To give him strength.

5 ASSETS

As the farm became more productive in the 1930s, Edward Sr. bought more tracts from Brooks. Each year he'd purchase a tract for one of his sons. For Moses, for Alex, for Sam, for Laighton, and on down the line until they all had a piece.

"We was all farming it together," said Scott. "We couldn't tell where one person's land was except by looking at the papers to see whose name was on it."

The boys were young. They didn't know what Edward Sr. knew. So they followed him and they learned. When Edward Sr. said it was time to chop cotton, they chopped cotton. When it was time to plow the corn and he said, "I want that corn wrapped up with dirt, now," the boys would plow.

"My daddy taught us all of that," Scott said. "He taught us everything about farming."

The corn crop Edward Sr. planted on one of his first tracts by the river fared much better than it had back in flooded Alabama. It grew faster than his teenage boys. More abundant than his wife's dinner table. It was almost too much corn. At harvest time, Edward Sr. rounded up all his sons and farmhands. They hauled corn for three weeks. Scott was still too small to do the hauling, but he rode on the wagon. His father asked them to load that wagon up with as much corn as they could carry and take up to the hills of Arkansas and sell it by the bushel. Moses, Laighton, and Alex, with little Scott sitting between them, sold every bit of it. "A thousand dollars in corn," tallied Edward Sr. after they got home. "Now I'm going to take this money and buy y'all five cultivators. I want to see my boys have five cultivators."

Edward Sr. took another load of corn to Memphis. He got all he could get out of it. With the money, he planned to get ten mules to go with those cultivators. When he got back home from Memphis he went to the mule man in Drew. He knew what he wanted. The color of the coats didn't matter. Whether the mules were Appaloosa or sorrel or patchwork gray. They could be any of those, or dirty white like an after-dinner dish towel if they had the temperament Edward Sr. needed: steady, calm, plodding, enduring, indestructible. He didn't have time for people or animals who lacked the mental toughness to stick it out until the last dying light. Maybe a mule as black as the Chevy. He did want to get one like that.

The mule man told Edward Sr. to take his pick, so he walked out and checked them over. He looked at their teeth. Found some that suited him.

"I've got eight hundred dollars here to pay on the mules," Edward Sr. said, walking back over to the mule man. He hoped to take the mules home that day.

The mule man nodded his approval. But he wouldn't accept all the cash. "You pay me five hundred now and take those mules and work them and pay the other when you get it." The mule man trusted Edward Sr., a man who kept his vows. And farmers with ambition, the mule man knew, almost always came back for more mules.

Every year, Edward Sr. sank his profits back into his operation. An investment in himself and his sons. He trained them, taught them what to grow and how to grow it. He timed them in the fields like an Olympic coach to see how quickly they could get a tight bale of hay. As the farm prospered, Edward Sr. moved dozens of sharecropper families onto his property to work it as paid laborers.

About then Edward Sr. began showing signs of liver failure; his legs swelled up at the end of the workday. To bring down the swelling, his wife and daughters heated up bags of cornmeal to lay across his legs as hot compresses. By morning he'd be ready to go again. When it got so bad he couldn't walk, he continued to farm, undaunted, from a chair in the yard. With binoculars, he supervised his sons and farmhands plowing up and down the rows. He'd see if someone plowed up some young cotton with the tractor or made any other mistake. He wouldn't say anything then, but he'd let the boys know when they got back from the fields that he'd been watching.

"[You knew] he was mad when he'd start working that nose like a rabbit," said Scott. "But he'd never curse. He'd just start working his nose like a rabbit until he'd be pleased with you."

Edward Sr. dressed each day in a starched and ironed suit of work clothes. If he got dirty in the field, he changed into a fresh set before heading into town. He was a businessman. He kept a frenetic pace, tending to every cornstalk and bean sprout and cotton tendril so that the final yield didn't only bring him even, but left enough extra to put back into the farm. Enough to keep growing.

Edward Sr. taught his sons that it wasn't a curse to be black. If visionaries led by example, he believed, others would see that success was possible. Scott collected these narratives and dismissed the notion that blackness was something tarnished.

He heard the same from one of the family's more eccentric neighbors, an old white man named Pap Smith who didn't farm or work, aside from plodding up the road on horseback every day greeting folks and making talk. Pap was a friend of Edward Sr.'s and liked to inquire about the state of the farm.

"What you think about this cotton?" Pap said one day as he passed by on horseback and saw that Edward Sr. was chopping cotton. "They said it's going to have the black root and die."

The black root was a soilborne pathogen that lived deep in the earth and wreaked havoc on crops. It could spread through a field and decimate, from the root up, vulnerable young cotton.

Edward Sr. stopped working and looked up. "What do you think about it?" he asked Pap.

Pap thought on it. Then he said that he knew a farmer who "been had the black root all his life and he's still living. Why the cotton got to die?"

With that, he turned the horse to leave. Taking their time, Pap and the horse ambled away up the roadside. After a while they disappeared behind the brambles.

6 WORK AND PLAY

Scott, a teenager, sat in the classroom of the high school run by Mr. Threadgill.[5] Scott got along well with Mr. Threadgill. "Ed, you ready today?" Mr. Threadgill asked.

"I sure ain't, now," little Scott replied.

Mr. Threadgill smiled. "Okay, well I'll pass you up today. You get your lessons tomorrow, then."

Instead of classwork, Scott and the others played. Played outside. Played with the girls. They had books, but they were tattered and out of date. They came used from the white schools and had missing pages and decade-old doodles.

In 1900, according to historian John Hope Franklin, an average of two dollars was spent on the education of a black child, compared with an average of three dollars for the education of a white child. By 1930 the separation had become a chasm. The same two dollars were spent on a black child while seven dollars were spent on the white child. Hope said this to a crowd at the University of Mississippi at an event of President Clinton's "One America in the 21st Century: The President's Initiative on Race."[6]

"It was as if," Franklin joked, "it took seven dollars to bring the backward white child up to the level of a black child, who could be educated for only two dollars. But that was not the case," Franklin continued, "and whites in power knew it. What they were aware of was a determination to replace slavery with a social and educational system that would hold blacks in a state of degradation and humiliation for an indefinite period of time. That would give whites in the twentieth century the same advantage that they enjoyed over blacks in the period of slavery. . . . Some of you may regard that as truly ancient history, but those of us who are still living and breathing in the shadow of such memories regard it as very, very contemporary."

The institutional priority for the education of Delta students of color throughout the twentieth century didn't appear to be appreciably different than it was at the end of the nineteenth. The problem was also obvious from the outside looking in. Between 1917 and 1932, Chicago philanthropist Julius Rosenwald, of the Sears, Roebuck fortune, joined with Booker T. Washington and others to help fund more than five thousand rural schoolhouses across the South for black children. Scott didn't attend one of these Rosenwald schools as a child, but one *was* built on Scott family land. When that historic school was closed, Scott's daughter Willena Scott-White said, it became an annex to the public T. Y. Fleming Elementary School in Leflore County, which Scott's grandson Daniel and his peers would attend in the 1970s. The promise of enlightenment had a hard time finding the boys and girls in the rural Delta. If Scott was to learn, he'd need to do it outside class.

Scott wasn't immediately concerned with mathematics or English composition. He was drawn to pragmatism and toil and mechanics, topics his textbooks never touched. He'd found work's purpose under the tutelage of his father; school was a luxury for the leisurely. It was the farm, which demanded discipline and physicality, that became his teacher.

Scott went as far as he could go at school, stopping at tenth grade. He had enjoyed shop class and taught himself to be a mechanic and a carpenter. Whenever he didn't know how to do something, he sought answers. "So I guess I didn't need those lessons no way," Scott reckoned.

7 NAMESAKE

Ed Scott, the seventh child, the fifth of six sons, was named after his father. It's unclear why Edward Sr. and Juanita didn't plaster the name on the first bare-bottomed boy who came into the world. Maybe Edward Sr. kept it holstered for the son he felt most akin to. Or maybe he and Juanita ran out of ideas after a while, having unloaded all those names on the ones who came before, including a few children who died in infancy.

"You never know why God let that last child be named Edward," said Rose Marie Scott-Pegues, Ed Scott's eldest daughter. "He was more like his father than any of [the other] children. [His] thing is, 'I don't want you to sell any of my land. Ever.' And I'm looking at this a million years from now. . . . This land will still be Scotts' land."[7]

When Edward Sr. got sick and was unable to work the land, it wasn't the elder Alex or Moses who picked up the torch, but Scott. Edward Sr. passed that authority down not by order of succession, but like water following the natural landscape.

"Ed, you're named after me, you got to work like me," Edward Sr. told his son early one workday. "You got to do everything I do."[8]

"All right, Daddy," Scott replied.

Scott's mother would pass in 1970. Her death scattered the holdings that Edward Sr. had amassed to his children and their descendants, many of whom had no interest in keeping it. Some of Scott's siblings convinced their mother to cut Scott out of the will. He has enough land, they argued. Some portions would be sold off within three months of Juanita's passing. Scott, by then a successful landowner in his own right, bought up all he could of the family plots from his siblings. But he wasn't able to get it all.

"He wanted that land because that was the land his father had started with," said Rose.

Long before he lost his parents, Scott saw the land as insurance for future generations, the only real commodity worth owning. It put him on equal footing alongside any other man, black or white, in the surrounding Delta. And that's really why Scott—like Edward Sr. before him—wore suits meticulously starched and creased. He was not just a field hand; he was the boss. His labor was black power, not black exploitation. The old story wasn't the only story.

8 HAND IN HAND

Ed Scott and his wife, Edna, met as teenagers. She lived in Mound Bayou, a predominantly black Delta town founded by freedmen in 1887 as a blank canvas for African American entrepreneurship and self-determination. Mound Bayou was fifteen miles west of Drew—close to the Scotts' Leflore County farm. Edna's father, Isaac Daniel, was also a farmer. He owned more than five hundred acres that he'd bought from white landowner Joe Rice Dockery. Like Scott's father, he'd started as a sharecropper.

Scott was fixated on Edna from the very first time he saw her in her father's yard in Mound Bayou. He was a strapping sixteen-year-old with a developing sense of purpose and a hat cocked slightly to the side that said the same. Arranged courtships were common then. Families who did business together or lived nearby played matchmaker. But Scott and Edna found each other. Scott, prospector that he was, saw in Edna the foundation he needed. He discovered her virtues: kindness, strength, faith and morality, a tittering laugh. But all that came later. On that first day, it was her beauty and graceful gait and made him say aloud, "That's a cute girl there. I'm going to go talk to her."

Scott made the trip to see Edna in Mound Bayou almost every Sunday. He'd arrive at the Daniels' house and sit and talk with Edna into the evening. When the sun started going down, Isaac Daniel would come into the living room, and Scott would know the visit was over even before Isaac Daniel said, "It's about to time to go to bed now."

(Years later, when his daughters dated, Scott was the protective father. He watched his daughters in the hallway mirror that he'd hung to give him a view from the kitchen into the living room. Once, when he saw a boy get too close to Willena, he charged in to tell them it was time for bed.)

Isaac Daniel was a strict father. But he came to consider Scott a son. His own sons had drifted away from the family and didn't have an interest in farming. In Delta agrarian life, a son meant extra hands and a vehicle for legacy. To Isaac Daniel, Scott was part of the bloodline. A marriage would connect for all time two of the area's few large-scale black farming families. But first, Scott would need to impress his bride.

Scott showed up for Edna one day without his hat. He'd left it on the foot of the bed where he put on his navy blue socks. Edna told him softly and directly that he had better go back and get his hat if he was going to take her out. "You can't go running around like a little boy with no hat on," she whispered. Scott went all the way back across the county line and got it.

They went on a drive into the lush and fiercely beautiful natural pockets of their Delta homeland. Scott drove one of his father's cars with the windows open. He drove as it pleased him, with no particular destination. Sometimes, his copilot, Edna, chimed in. Why don't you turn that way? I wonder what's down that road there? That's how they found the blackberry patch.

Scott's favorite dessert was blackberry pie, and it all started here. That simple dish was soaked sweet with the innocence and the open road of youth. Scott and Edna picked the fragile berries. He took off his button-up and used it like a basket. Some blackberries burst in the pile and stained Scott's white shirt like blood. Before much longer the blackberries would be gone, overripe or picked clean by birds. To get enough for a pie they had to be quick. They gathered as many as they could carry. Scott glimpsed a giant ripe cluster near the ground and bent down to pick. Edna held the branches back to shield him from the thorns.

On the way home in the Chevrolet, Scott lost control around a curve. They careened into the underbrush and hit a small tree. Scott's hat flew off his head, bounced off the windshield, and landed on the floor. He turned to Edna and asked if she was all right. She nodded, sitting neatly in the seat with her hands in her lap. The wreck dented the front end, and the car was stranded. Scott stepped out. Edna handed him his hat off the floorboard and he set it on his head. Then she grabbed the shirt full of blackberries and got out of the car. Scott took her hand, and they set off down the road together toward home.

9   IN THE DITCH

Scott lay face down in the ditch with General George S. Patton, Old Blood and Guts himself. It was early 1945 on the edge of the Western Front. Allied troops under Patton's command had moved into Germany and kicked the door off the hinges. The German forces that remained were scattered. The most dangerous, Scott said, were the lone pilots who hid their planes in woodland brush and would swoop out of the sky without warning to rain bullets down on convoys. Watching the horizon line, Scott imagined snipers in their crevices, doing without orders from their commanders and proper food of any kind for weeks, but being too far in to turn back, licking their cracked lips and shouldering their rifles and hoping to find some moral sustenance in the form of enemy servicemen (or officers, praise be!) centered in their sights. It was a German sniper who now had Patton and Scott pinned down. Scott had been driving gasoline trucks from France out here to the front lines these past months and had been tapped to drive Patton's Jeep on this routine recon mission, but then the shots came skidding across the bow of the Jeep from the bell tower of a church about a half mile away. The general went overboard to find cover. Scott scrambled after him.

The action Scott saw in the war came like that—suddenly. He and the other soldiers would be polishing equipment or looking at maps or driving unimpeded through the countryside when bullets or barked orders or a bombshell shattered the fourth wall and put their boot camp rehearsals to the test. Instincts took over. Their training had been about repetition. Mental protocols. Navigation. Evasion. Chain of command. Personal hygiene. The mantras and exercises became so mundane that the men didn't even think about them anymore. They internalized them and, when it came time, leaned on them for survival. Lying there in the ditch, Scott knew enough to keep his head down. It was a trick he'd learned. Keep focused on your mission and don't let the other man see you coming.

There was silence after the first shot. Patton looked up at the sky. Not a cloud; nothing. He directed his attention through his tilted ear, listening. Scott gripped his .45 out of habit. In his other hand he held the radio he'd grabbed out of the Jeep when he bailed. After a minute of unbroken stillness Patton looked over at Scott. "You're alright, soldier," Scott recalled Patton saying. Scott didn't know if it was a question or an order. "I am," he replied.

10 PARACHUTE

Scott had enlisted in 1942 when he was twenty years old. He had hoped to be a paratrooper, to see the world from way up high where the air got thin, to float down like dandelion fluff and land neatly on the earth again. But when he got to Camp Shelby, Mississippi, for basic training, he saw the paratroopers training. They were dropped off a tall tower, their chutes slowing the descent just enough so they didn't hit the ground like bricks. It wasn't the picture that Scott had of heroic men coasting through the clouds like on the war bond ads in the post office back home. "When I got down to Camp Shelby and saw those people turning them loose and they'd fall eighty or ninety feet in the air—going *whoosh*—I said aw Lord, I don't want to be no paratrooper."

Instead, Scott spent time with the jeeps, the big trucks, the engines. Everybody talked about killing Nazis, but Scott figured none of that could happen without tune-ups and fresh tires. And he was right. Scott became a quartermaster, designated to haul cargo and cart officers around, which he did often on base. He left Camp Shelby and went to Camp Croft in South Carolina. It was one step closer to the coastline and the big ships that carried men to the other side of the Atlantic. The monotony of basic kept the war's terrifying realities at bay. After all, Scott was still on southern soil, with no certainty of his next posting. In camp, his anxieties were more immediate, like his fear of needles. On immunization day, Scott lined up with the rest of the soldiers for shots. In through the back door of the clinic; it felt to him like a march to slaughter. Inch by inch, man by man, into the chute. Scott, petrified, followed them inside. But it was essential, just like basic training was. Everything they needed to survive. "We didn't know then that we were going overseas," Scott said. "But we were."

He was proud of his Army obligations. His truck was as dear to him as the tractor and the Chevy back home. He shined it with a rag soaked in linseed oil. The officers who piled in to be driven to their classes on base admired its gleam.

One afternoon, an officer came over to Scott while he was polishing the tires. "Oh, you got a good-looking truck," he said, looking down at Scott with his thumbs in the waistband. "What did you do to it?"

Scott, rag in hand, told him it was linseed oil and elbow grease.

Overseas, the conflict raged. The Army needed supplies and quartermasters. The officers knew things the soldiers didn't know. Like how soon they would be whisked away from the regular showers and meals on base to the uncertain accommodations of war-torn Europe.

Furloughs were a common reward for soldiers who had completed basic training. Officers handed them out to men who impressed the brass. Scott got his three-day furlough because of his perseverant good humor and the shine of his truck. He made good use of his last three days in the country. He went home and married Edna.

Edward Sr. wasn't told about the wedding plans until the last minute. Scott's mother had kept it a secret. It was her job, not Edward Sr.'s, to look out for her son's heart, and she knew Edna had taken charge of that long ago.

"Edward's talking about marrying that little girl," she told her husband a few weeks before the wedding.

"What little girl?!" Edward Sr. asked.

"Mr. Daniel's daughter," she said.

Edward Sr. nodded in acceptance. "I didn't know nothing about that, now."

Scott married Edna at the Bolivar County courthouse in Cleveland. When they couldn't get a commitment from the pastor at their home church, they did with whatever clergy they could manage. "We met a man on the street and asked him about marrying us," said Scott. "Don't know to this day who he was. He was supposed to have been a preacher." The stranger-preacher recited verses out of a pocket Bible at the ceremony. Scott gave him a few dollars for his trouble. The preacher couldn't write, and Scott and Edna coached him through filling in the blanks on the marriage license. Scott left town a day later to get back to South Carolina. Edna was the last to tell him goodbye before he got on the bus. He played with his wedding ring for the whole trip. The gold band wasn't much, but it made Scott feel strong.

11 MIDDLE PASSAGE

Scott's unit was headed to France. He was among an all-black group of Army quartermasters whose job it would be to resupply the Allied front lines. Their job was vital. They were skilled and brave. But the Army's institutional distrust of black soldiers persisted; the brass were reluctant to assign black commanding officers to this black troop. The soldiers, however, had leverage. Before they left for war, Scott and his comrades had insisted that they stay with the black officers who had been training alongside them. "If you take the black officers we're all going AWOL," Scott remembered the soldiers saying. They weren't joking. The commanders gave in. The successful resistance was revelatory for Ed Scott, who would go on to challenge conventions back in the Delta. Standing up to authority wasn't foolish and ignorant, as he'd been told. The prospect of abduction and lynching on dark Mississippi roads—the consequence for breaking social codes—had always given him pause. But he thought now that it might be the white bosses who were afraid of him.

The battle tactics that Scott honed in the military would serve double duty all his life. You can better defend against your enemies in a firefight from an elevated position, he learned. Just like you could seize a sociological advantage by fighting injustice from moral high ground. His father's teachings already coursed through him. War cemented Scott's form.

As far as Scott knew, his troop was the only one in the brigade to retain black representation through the ranks. He imagined there was a betting pool. An over/under on how many of these Negro truck drivers without white leaders at the helm would die. "We'll see how it comes out," Scott overheard a white officer say.

The men left New York by ship in the fall of 1944. They crossed the Atlantic for France over the same waters that had made American colonization and slavery possible centuries before. The soldiers' passage was comfortable compared with the historical accommodations of desperate emigrants—fleeing by choice—and the captured slaves from West Africa—forcefully transported by way of the Caribbean tropics to the American South. Scott ate three meals a day and moved freely on deck atop the ghosts of those lost in these waters, who would have traveled cramped in the hold or, if they fell ill from typhoid or diphtheria, been thrown off the side into the waves. Scott thought he could hear gurgling gasps coming from the ship's whitewater wake.

Scott wondered how the black men would be treated on foreign soil. Would he ever make it home? Would he end up dead and buried in an unmarked grave? Or discarded with no resting place at all? Scott found comfort in the collective purpose, white and black banded together as fighting men—in ways they could not have been as civilians back home—against a fascist threat that targeted them all. The troops landed in the port city of Marseille, recently reclaimed by the Allies as part of Operation Dragoon, which followed on the heels of Normandy. Marseille was a key port and the largest city in France outside of Paris.

Scott and the troops remained on board the ship in port for two days, awaiting final operational preparations. Scott looked out from the deck and saw, for the first time, a country not his own. Beyond the harbor lay a whole civilization, steeped in its own long history, with its own stories and languages and culture. America seemed young and inexperienced by contrast, the span of Mississippi history so much more truncated. Europe was a land of castles and lineage. Not like the Delta, which was flat and stunted and still in seed.

An officer spoke to the soldiers standing on the dock as the ship pulled away. Scott saw the smoke billow from the stack and knew he wasn't going back. "Let me tell you about those barracks and the women over there," the officer told them. "There are ten thousand licensed whores over there. If you get caught . . . you're going to the stockade."

The men stood firm in formation.

"We were afraid to go over there. Nice-looking building, women all the way up to the top, hanging out the window with nothing on," remembered Scott.

High-end hotels, forsaken by their owners and guests during the war, had been remade as high-rise brothels. The Nazis formalized prostitution in Europe's captured cities, but after Allied forces regained control in Marseille, a contingent of willing businesswomen remained. As sex workers have for centuries, they capitalized on the anxieties and appetites of fearful soldiers. The men came for fleeting carnal life before facing a thousand possible deaths in the field. When Scott and his quartermasters walked the streets below the brothels, women hung out the windows. In broken English, the sirens cooed. *Sucky sucky.* Scott kept moving.

White officers spread a rumor in the French-speaking tenements that black American soldiers were not like their fair-skinned counterparts. They whispered that black men were part animal. "Them niggers got tails," Scott remembered the officers saying.

When Scott had cause to visit local homes, the French residents tried to peek behind to catch a look at his tail. "Where are you going to sit down?" the French asked.

12 ALONE ON THE ROAD

General Patton's Third Army advanced across the Western Front beginning in August 1944 and all the way through spring of 1945, when the German military was in its final death throes. With few exceptions, Patton moved quickly and brazenly, racking up victories through France and Belgium and Germany and anywhere his boots fell. He helped secure victory at the Battle of the Bulge in December 1944 on the rough terrain of the Ardennes Forest; it was the largest battle of the war and a decisive turning point. Between August 1, 1944, and the end of the fighting on May 8, 1945, Patton and his men claimed to have captured, wounded, or killed more than 1.5 million Nazis—6 enemy combatants for every U.S. soldier in the ranks.[9] Patton abandoned nearly all defensive strategies on his hunt for German forces. He rolled over Nazi encampments and liberated or captured cities with equal parts nimbleness and brute force. The Army set up fueling stations and depots as fast as possible to keep Patton supplied. The only thing that could slow the Third Army down was lack of fuel.

The Third Army was the tip of the spear, which meant they often shivered in the cold, low on gas and supplies at critical moments. This is where Scott and the quartermasters came in. Scott drove truckloads of gasoline (and equipment and rations and pairs of woolen gloves) deep into the fray, through regions steamrolled by the Allies but not yet fully secured. American soldiers stationed on the highways waved these trucks through, pointing them toward the safe routes and away from the little towns still dotted with German infantry.

According to Maj. Gen. Robert McGowan Littejohn, chief quartermaster for the European theater at the time, the essentials of war were men, guns, airplanes, shipping, and food. (Littlejohn, as it happened, was a dear friend of Patton's and was a pallbearer at his funeral.) The rations that Scott and the other quartermasters delivered (and ate) weren't comparable to dinner on the farm, but they weren't as bad as they had been in the first few years of the war, when American soldiers complained of the British fare they were forced to down. The Army used British flour made of local soft wheat, Canadian wheat, and a little barley and oats for the bread ration. It made a dark loaf that didn't satisfy American soldiers. Littlejohn and his Army cooks and nutritionists went to work. After much trial and error, they'd done it: rolls and biscuits that tasted quite a lot like the ones back home. "Our ration in the European Theatre of Operations is excellent," Littlejohn reported. "With a minimum of shipping we have a ration equal, if not superior, to that of any other place in the world." Littlejohn's confidence in his product makes him sound like Ed Scott. The quartermasters were saviors. Wherever Scott arrived, fuel tanks ranneth over and the men had their biscuits.[10]

Scott drove deep into France. Along the way he spent two weeks at a fueling station sleeping on hay and waiting for his orders. Then, his truck stocked with drums of gasoline, he jumped back into his seat in the cab. His truck, like many in the convoy, was one of the Dodge wc series that Patton preferred because of its performance on the makeshift roads. With the French rail system decimated, trucks were the only means of transport.

The Army dubbed one of Patton's key supply lines in 1944 the Red Ball Express, a term the Santa Fe Railroad originated in the late nineteenth century to give priority to trains carrying perishable cargo.[11] Each of the Red Ball trucks was painted with a red circle, as were the road signs that guided their way. Following D-Day, the route stretched across France on the heels of the advancing Third Army.

During this period Scott drove nonstop, his headlights dimmed to avoid detection. In all, the 28 divisions along the Western Front needed more than 750 tons of supplies per day. In a letter to "The Officers and Men of the Red Ball Highway," General Eisenhower described "The Red Ball Line" as "the lifeline between combat and supply. To it falls the tremendous task of getting vital supplies from ports and depots to the combat troops, when and where such supplies are needed, material without which the armies might fail." And the majority of the truck drivers traveling the Red Ball Express—as many as five thousand every twenty-four hours—were African Americans.[12]

"It was mostly black men who drove the Red Ball Express," said another black veteran who traversed the route. "We were all eighteen and nineteen. . . . We were so young; we didn't think we would ever die."[13]

On that day and every day, Scott joined the long line of the convoy. The flagman waved them through, and they were off. It was cold. A few trucks got stuck in the mud and then froze in their tracks. Men got trench foot and had to pull off to wait for medics in jeeps to cart them back to the field hospital. New trucks came with new drivers with dry boots.

The road was harsh. During one run, a driver lost control of his truck when he stepped out on the running board to pee. The truck flipped over and rolled off the road into a ditch. Drums of gasoline came loose and crashed down on top of him. Scott was sure that "crazy boy" was dead. When they got to him, though, he was moaning, miraculously still alive. "When they got him out of there they carried him to the hospital and we didn't see him no more."

You had to be a little crazy to do the job. It was about focusing your energy, suspending disbelief, and embracing the otherworldliness of the task at hand. On the long runs through the countryside, engine rumbling beneath him, Scott went back to the fields of Mississippi. He rolled his window down in the brutal cold so he could stick his arm out like he used to do. These moments would inevitably be interrupted by a blown-out tire or gunfire that ricocheted off the road, dangerously close to the combustible cargo.

At the fuel depot, the chatter through the convoy had been all about how Patton and his men were kicking ass out there. The drivers knew they were a part of the action, even when the battle was miles away. Sometimes it was closer. Before the convoy pulled out, Scott discovered he had a flat tire. The company commander took a look. "Mr. Scott, you know the way?" he asked.

"Yeah, I know the way," Scott replied. "But those people are going to be out there shooting at me."

"No," the commander said. "We're going to take care of you."

Back on the road again, Scott was making up for lost time. He came to a guard station at the fork in the road. "I guess this guard was sleeping," Scott recalled, "because he didn't tell me nothing, and I drove right on into a town [that I shouldn't have been in]."

Scott wheeled into the empty village and lit up a row of darkened houses with his headlights. He paused and listened. Then the gunshots came. Bullets pelted the truck, clanging against the metal in a frightening drumbeat. Scott wheeled the clumsy truck around in the thoroughfare as gunfire dimpled the door. He was afraid to look out into the dark windows, lit up in a blaze of automatic weapons. He thought about the previous occupants; imagined them still there, huddling under the kitchen table while the firing Nazis used their couch cushions as sandbags. Scott turned the wheel again. He was almost out. He prayed the cargo wouldn't explode. *What was the nature of this Nazi hate? Did those men inside the dark room hate him just for being American? Or did they just think they were doing their jobs?* Scott hit the gas hard and skidded away, back up toward the fork, chased by bullets. He roared past the guard station, still empty. He would have to find his own way.

13   FIREFIGHT

Scott finally caught up to the convoy. They traveled by the light of the moon, nearly full, which was "shining like the daylight." At a bend in the road the convoy screeched to a stop. All fifteen trucks in the group hit the brakes. A driver up ahead yelled for everybody to stay put—"I heard the boy say, 'Wait, wait, wait.'"

A rogue Nazi pilot was gunning for them, perhaps hoping for a kill to justify the loss of his brothers and his own leaking wounds, open sores, and pain-wracked stomach. On his first approach the pilot tore up the road, but he didn't have his aim quite right.

One of the quartermasters said they should stay quiet, not fire back and risk giving away their position. But Scott knew, with the moon "bright-bright" as it was, that there was no concealing their whereabouts. Scott's truck carried a mounted .50-caliber rifle. He jumped out of his cab and got behind his artillery. "I don't care what they say, if he comes back shooting at us, I'm going to shoot."

The men saw the way-up plane pass across the moon's glow. Passing, as Scott described it, "between the moon and the moonlight." Other quartermasters had taken up their guns, too. They pointed them skyward and waited for the plane's descent. The pilot was circling, adjusting his bead. Then he took the plunge.

The quartermasters waited for the precise moment. The guns were loaded with tracer rounds that would light up the night like roman candles, all the way to the target. Just before the plane unleashed its payload, the truckers let fly. Scott kept his sights on the moving plane as the .50 caliber rocked and kicked like an angry washing machine. The sky, on fire.

The plane pulled out of its descent to avoid the shelling and flew back over the trees. "He gone?" one man asked.

After a minute, they saw a red blaze over in the distance. "He crashed over there!" yelled another.

"Well that's good," was all Scott said as he climbed back into the cab. It had been his first time to shoot back at the enemy. A turning point in what would be a lifetime of self-defense.

14 ALLIED POWER

Patton's forces had advanced into Germany by February 1945. The Nazis were on the run, desperate and dangerous. The Third Army had pushed into the German Saarland and was awaiting resupply. The general sent about half of his troops back for rest, telling them, Scott remembered, to "drink as much whiskey as you want, but be ready when I call you."

Leaning against his truck at the depot, Scott shivered in the freezing air. He talked with a road guard who couldn't stop going on about how cold his hands were without gloves. The guard had lost them a few days back, he said, and hadn't found any replacements. He'd been burying his hands in his pockets to try to keep them from freezing, unwilling to take them out if he could help it, to the point that instead of directing traffic with looping hand movements, he'd gotten to just nodding his head this way and that like he was greeting a stranger on the sidewalk. The guard told Scott they were getting ready to move Patton's headquarters back off the front lines because it seemed the Germans weren't going to be putting up any fight. As they were talking, Scott saw General

Patton about a hundred yards away, conversing outside a tent with some officers.

Patton had received some intelligence, Scott would later gather. The Germans were making a final stand. Backed into a corner, troops that had been chased out of a dozen nearby cities banded together. With more than half of Patton's men back on rest, the Germans, weakened as they were in morale and ammunition, outnumbered the present U.S. force. And they were on the march. Scott heard a man yell in Patton's direction, "Are we still going to move those headquarters?"

"Hell no," Patton said. "I'm going to hold the line."

As Scott remembered it, eight of the nine divisions had been sent back to rest. Miles away and likely a few drinks deep. Patton got on the radio and ordered every man back—"Right now! Every troop down there, whether you're sober or drunk, come to the front line. . . . And when you get there, come out shooting!"

An officer approached Scott and the other drivers. He asked how much action they'd seen. They said they'd seen some. He told them, darting away, that they'd be seeing more soon enough.

Scott and the quartermasters felled huge trees with explosives to block the roadway and slow the Germans down. The divisions that had been sent back for rest were storming back toward the front lines. Instead of joining the existing force, they flanked the enemy. When the fighting started, the Germans were blindsided. "When [our boys] got behind them they were being shot at from the front and the back," said Scott. "They wanted to get out of there then. Next thing we saw was taillights going back up the highway. The white flag came out about two o'clock." Not long after, Patton requested a recon escort.

Scott and Patton, back in the ditch. They lay low, ducking sniper fire that seemed to be coming simultaneously from everywhere and nowhere in particular. Patton had been first to fall into the ditch. He yelled back at Scott to follow his lead. "In the ditch, boy! In the ditch!" Scott came around the back of the truck so he didn't walk into the sniper's sight line.

Patton peeked out with his binoculars long enough to see where the shots were coming from. The sniper was holed up in the bell tower of a not-so-distant church, one of the few buildings still standing, and one of the tallest structures in the area. It had proved a sanctuary for the sharpshooters. The church was some 250 yards from the ditch. Patton told Scott to give him the walkie-talkie and called back to base.

"He used his radio," said Scott, "and called the Crazy T.D.s."

The Crazy T.D.s were a tight-knit "bunch of black boys that shot field artillery," Scott recalled. Brash braggarts. T.D. stood for "tank destroyer," the M36 Tank Destroyer. It carried the latest artillery that could penetrate the armor of German Panther and Tiger tanks. The Crazy T.D.s scorched the earth with these machines.

It's likely that the Crazy T.D.s in Scott's story were part of the 761st Tank Battalion, also known as the "Black Panther" Battalion. The Army was still formally segregated during World War II, and the 761st served under Patton on the Western Front just as Scott did. Patton maintained rigid opinions about the superiority of the white race—they were smarter and more capable to lead, he thought—but he appreciated the spirit of the black soldiers and the Crazy T.D.s, who answered the call when he demanded manpower and courage.

Patton had addressed the 761st as a group when they first joined the fighting months before. He impressed on them the importance of their positions as the first Negro tankers to ever fight in the American Army. The entire black race was watching them, he said. Looking to their great success. They better not let their brothers and sisters down. And more important, damn it, they better not let him down. "I would never have asked for you if you weren't good. . . . I don't care what color you are as long as you go up there and kill those Kraut sons of bitches."[14]

When the Crazy T.D.s got the orders from Patton, they were thirteen miles from the Jeep and the ditch. They heard the gruff, urgent voice of their general crackling through the walkie-talkie and jumped into action.

Patton relayed the coordinates and the elevation of the church. Scott waited. A few moments of silence stretched on until Scott heard the ominous whistling in the air. Risking a glance, Patton and Scott looked out over the top of the ditch. The first round went long, exploding craters on a sloping hill fifty yards behind the church.

"Go back and try again," Patton said into the radio. "You've got to draw your elevation in."

The next missile went just over the spire of the church.

"You're coming close," Patton relayed. "Now you need to shoot for effect . . . shoot for effect!"

The Crazy T.D.s launched a third volley that hit the church dead center, just above the front door, where parishioners would have entered. The building buckled as though its beams and joists had suddenly turned into pudding. Patton told the T.D.s to drop another shell in there. "You're hitting it just right now!" he yelled.

After the next shot, there was quiet. Scott and Patton cautiously stood up and brushed themselves off. "That's the last we saw of that church or anybody in it," remembered Scott. After the war, whenever Scott heard civil rights activists speak of "black power," he was reminded of the Crazy T.D.s leveling the enemy's church with their shells.

15 COMING HOME

The train was packed with soldiers. The war was over. The transport arrived on U.S. soil triumphantly. The men piled off the ship and began the journey home, some destined for little towns in Kentucky, others for Tennessee, Texas, Arkansas, Alabama, California—and Scott to Mississippi. Scott first returned to Camp Croft in South Carolina, where he boarded a train headed west. There were so many of them on board, Scott said, that their locomotive struggled to make it over the Appalachian foothills. "They had to cut some of them [cars] loose and make two trips."

Station after station, men off-loaded and set off for their respective homesteads, changing trains, hopping buses, flagging cabs, following the winding American circuitry that took them down the ever-narrowing boulevards and avenues and dirt roads to their front doors. Columbus, Mississippi, was Scott's final stop by train. He carried his duffel to a bench and sat down to wait for a Greyhound to Greenwood. He was still wearing his uniform. He held his hat in his hand. When the bus arrived, he got in line to board. The man checking tickets stuck his palm out wordlessly. *Step back.* Scott waited as the ticket taker waved white folks and civilians on ahead of him. When he saw a break in the line, he jumped in, telling the man, "Take the damn ticket. I'm getting on this bus *now*."

"[The people back home] didn't care about us no way," Scott said, speaking of whites' reception of black veterans. "They didn't want to see you with that uniform on back then. I was proud of that uniform, but I wasn't proud of Mississippi. Wasn't proud of Mississippi at all."

James Baldwin identified the treatment of black soldiers as a turning point in American race relations:

A certain hope died. . . . You must put yourself in the skin of a man who is wearing the uniform of his country, is a candidate for death in its defense, and who is called a "nigger" by his comrades-in-arms and his officers; who is almost always given the hardest, ugliest, most menial work to do; who knows that the white G.I. has informed the Europeans that he is subhuman. . . . And who, at the same time, as a human being, is far freer in a strange land than he has ever been at home. Home! The very word begins to have a despairing and diabolical ring. . . . And all this is happening in the richest and freest country in the world, and in the middle of the twentieth century.[15]

Scott thought about leaving Mississippi for good. But he saw his father was sick, no longer able to run the farm by himself. Edward Sr. wanted his son to go back to school, but Scott said no. He already had a vocation in mind. And a purpose. His destiny was to be tied up in the dirt, with his father's. "You can't work this place like you're doing by yourself," he told his father. "I'm going to stay right here with you, Daddy."

16 BOSS

Scott drove his father's '47 Chevrolet pickup. The dirt roads were pot-holed, and he was careful not to go too fast until he got back on the blacktop. He was carrying a family of sharecroppers. His father had sent Scott to pick them up and bring them back to the farm so they could start a new life. Not everyone could own their own farm, Scott knew, but all deserved a chance at dignified labor. Edward Sr. taught his son that a bounty of work was the real blessing, and a moral businessman was one who shared the fruits of his enterprise.

It was early morning. Edward Sr. had sent the check ahead of time to settle the sharecroppers' score with the plantation owner. When Scott pulled up in front of the shack the family was standing out on the crooked porch, bags packed. A spindly man, his rotund wife, and their two boys and one daughter. One of the boys was strapping. The other was a runt; he needed to "put some more bricks in his britches," as a local saying went.

The wife and daughter rode up front with Scott. The men sat in the open truck bed with their belongings. In the rearview mirror Scott saw the men staring back at their former home as it got smaller and smaller until it disappeared entirely. Then they gazed at that spot in the distance where the plantation had been, beyond their sight but still firmly in their minds. The mother looked exhausted, as if she'd just set down a heavy load. She never looked back from the front seat, just stared at the road as it turned from dirt to gravel to pavement. She watched the yellow lines blur down the center and didn't say much.

Scott blew out a tire as they got close to home. He and the boys changed it on the roadside. They got to the Scott farm before noon. Edward Sr. greeted them and had the family shown to their house. He told Scott to take the truck to get it looked at.

The Scotts were Chevrolet men. Chevys were all they ever bought. And they bought a lot of them. The GM plant in Detroit knew Edward Sr. per-sonally because he insured so many vehicles with the company. A man named Mr. Johnny ran the local dealership that serviced all of Edward Sr.'s trucks. Johnny was out to lunch and late getting back when Scott arrived that day to see him. Scott told the woman at the desk that he'd just wait. He sat down.

A man named Bob who worked in the repair shop saw Scott waiting and came over. He was with another man named Frank. "What you waiting on, Ed?!" Bob said, louder than necessary.

Scott didn't respond at first. As polite as business-savvy Johnny was to the Scotts, a few of the other employees didn't seem to like them much. "Ed, I'm talking to you," Bob repeated.

"I'm waiting on Mr. Johnny," said Scott. "My daddy sent me out here with this truck and told me to have him check it. It ain't been checked."

Frank got mad. He started yelling. Scott didn't recall every word. Could have been something like: *You think we work for you?! We're not going to check that piece of shit every time a bug hits the windshield. We're not going to keep it up for you and your daddy if y'all can't do it!*

Scott left immediately. On the way home, he cried. He felt small, like he had as a boy. As if the whole world was tilted against folks like him. By the time he got home he had put this feeling out of his mind. His tears had dried. He was just mad.

Edward Sr. looked puzzled when his son pulled in so soon. "What's your trouble, boy?" he asked. The men at the shop had cussed him, Scott told his father.

Edward Sr.'s face changed. "Get my car out of the shed," he instructed. Scott pulled the Chevy around. Edward Sr. came out of the house with his Winchester rifle in one hand and a pistol in the other. He put his rifle in the backseat and got into the passenger side with his pistol on his lap. Scott had the truck idling. "Take me to Drew," his father said. "I'm tired of people running over my children."

Johnny was back in the office when Scott and Edward Sr. arrived. Edward Sr. got out of the car, pistol bulging in his pocket. "Mr. Johnny, I need to see you," he said, "and Mr. Frank and Mr. Bob."

Johnny went into the shop to get the others. When the three of them came back, Edward Sr. took the stage.

"I just bought it from you last week!" railed Edward Sr., "and y'all cuss my son and tell him you ain't going to check that damn truck every time it needs checking. . . . I don't cuss my children and I ain't going to have you cussing them."

Bob and Frank stared at their shoes like scolded children. Edward Sr. pierced them with his eyes.

"Johnny, you need to get word to them," Edward Sr. said. "Have them understand. Please don't cuss my children out here no more or I'll go somewhere else to trade. . . . And any time you get ready to kick one of my children or cuss one of them, come kick or cuss me. I'm an older man, I can take it."

Johnny nodded sheepishly and extended his hand to Edward Sr. He had a few private words with Bob and Frank. As the Scotts were going back to the car, they passed by the finance office. A lady behind a desk saw them go by and hollered out after them, "When are you going to pay something on your bill?"

Edward Sr. stopped and looked at his son. He turned around and walked to the open door of the finance office and leaned in at the lady. Mr. Johnny saw it and came over frantically. "Mr. Johnny, you ought to tell that lady who I am," said Edward Sr. "If I make a bill I'm going to pay it the next week. Evidently she doesn't know me. . . . I ain't going to make a bill and not pay it."

Edward Sr. turned on the toe of his shoe and walked out. Scott heard the lady yelling back at Johnny. "Well I didn't know who he was! He's a black man, I thought he owed a bill out here!"

The Scotts didn't owe anyone anything.

17 PUNY COTTON

After the war, Scott bought 160 acres from Edward Sr. In the family tradition, the Scotts farmed their collective holdings as one entity. Edward Sr. directed the planting and harvesting, and Scott executed his orders. Scott was the son most drawn to agricultural work. Moses, the eldest brother, didn't have the same passion for farming. Laighton died an early death from complications during an eye surgery in Chicago. Sam remarried and moved to Cleveland, Ohio, after his first wife committed suicide; soon after, disillusioned and homesick, he shot himself outside a Cleveland police station. Scott's younger brother, Harvey, aspired to a life beyond the farm. Only Alex, nine years older, still worked the land. He had fallen in love with hogs. Alex knew his hundreds of pigs by name. He'd notice if even one spotted sow went missing. Scott and his father carried on planting vast fields of cotton and soybeans, and soon, rice.

In 1947 Edward Sr. was among the first in the area to embrace rice. They seeded the fields below the house, but until they could put in a well, there was no way to irrigate. Scott recalled that his father splashed water out of a ditch onto the crop to make it grow. When they finally dug a well, they installed ditches to transport the water, aqueducts of Delta clay.

The Scotts were doing well. The land Edward Sr. had amassed bore fruit. Edna Scott would indirectly bring the next big entrepreneurial opportunity for the family. Edna's father, Isaac Daniel, owned 510 acres in Mound Bayou. He fell into debt and, with nowhere to turn for help, looked to the farming expertise of his son-in-law.

Isaac Daniel, Scott saw, was clearly in over his head. He had more debt than he could manage and more land than he had resources to farm. And Scott saw something even more fundamental. The cotton crop wasn't yielding as much as it should. Isaac Daniel wasn't farming it right.

Isaac Daniel was hardheaded. Scott couldn't simply correct his father-in-law; he had to lead by example. In the first few years of the 1960s, Scott farmed as much in Mound Bayou with Isaac Daniel as he did with Edward Sr. over in nearby Leflore County. Scott told Daniel that if he was going to try to turn the operation around, he needed some of that land to farm on his own. "I need to work it by myself," he insisted. Isaac Daniel agreed.

The land Isaac Daniel worked stretched from Mound Bayou all the way up to nearby Shelby. He gave Scott free run of some of those fields and farmed the others as he always had. Scott seeded. Isaac Daniel seeded. They had set up a perfect experiment to test Scott's hypothesis. Same weather, same equipment, different schools of thought.

Both men had cotton bolls spring forth right on schedule. But Scott's were heartier, as white and fluffy as sheep's curls. When it was nearing harvest time, Isaac Daniel looked in awe at what the young man had made. He wondered why Scott's bolls were so much bigger than his mal-nourished flock.

It was the best year Scott ever had in cotton. Armed with exhibit A, he turned to Isaac Daniel, who'd been plowing the other fields as he'd always done. And doing it all wrong, according to Scott. There was a way to clear away the weeds from cotton that didn't sever the roots of the young plants. But Isaac Daniel had insisted on plowing too close. "Oh, no, we got to get the grass out, we got to get the grass out," Scott impersonated him.

Even if the weeds were gone and the field looked clean, the cotton would have been disturbed. A farmer wouldn't see the fault in the method until months later when the cotton yield was puny. Scott plowed with surgical precision. He snatched the weeds from around the crop, the blades just an inch away, and left the cotton alone to grow.

Scott wasn't born knowing how to farm, but he was born to parents who had knowledge to pass down. He, in turn, was open with what he knew. That had always been one of the black farmer's biggest roadblocks. The powerful had the road map to success, but in the status quo South, they didn't like to share.

Isaac Daniel stood in Scott's field with wonderment on his face. He reached down and took one of the healthy, fluffy bolls in his hand. He squeezed it, comprehending at last.

18 MORAL FIBER

In 1887, freedmen founded Mound Bayou in the aftermath of the Civil War. The town's story began when wealthy slave owner Joseph Davis, brother of Confederate president Jefferson Davis, sold land to for-mer slave Benjamin Montgomery. Montgomery founded an all-black town near Vicksburg called Davis Bend. Benjamin Montgomery's son, Isaiah T. Montgomery, became a driving force in this utopian project. When Davis Bend ultimately failed, Isaiah Montgomery and his cousin Benjamin Green moved a hundred or so miles north and led the found-ing of Mound Bayou in what had been a blank slate of Delta wild. Like many farmers and builders of that time, Isaiah Montgomery and his supporters carved homes, farmland, and community out of the unforgiving bottomlands. Long before government policies addressed the systemic racism of the Old South, Mound Bayou's intelligentsia and professional class achieved an autonomous and self-governed black idyll.[16]

Mound Bayou thrived in the early 1900s. Smartly dressed black doctors arrived in town at the busy rail depot. Heels clicked past the Royal Club, which served wine and beer, on the way to an evening at the Lyceum Theater.[17] Children played in the streets after school; the town, with the help of advocates such as Booker T. Washington, had a well-run network of public and private schools. The land in Mound Bayou that Isaac Daniel owned and Scott farmed was an extension of this pioneering project.

In the 1940s, the Knights and Daughters of Tabor funded a hospital in Mound Bayou that revolutionized access to top-notch services for African Americans in the region. Chief Surgeon T. R. M. Howard became a heroic healthcare provider and community organizer. Dr. Howard also farmed in Mound Bayou and opened a restaurant, a zoo, an insurance company, and the first swimming pool for blacks in Mississippi. He used his influence in the private sector to fight for social progress, voter registration, and human rights.[18] Many in that tight-knit community, including Dr. Howard, knew that their progressiveness made them targets. Mound Bayou's self-governance included self-defense, and the town developed a reputation as an ironclad haven. If you were a sympathetic soul being chased down Highway 61 by the Klan, your best option was to roar across the city line into fortified Mound Bayou where the Klan dared not stop.

In the aftermath of the infamous Emmett Till murder in nearby Money, Mississippi, in 1955, Dr. Howard stood alongside naacp Mississippi field secretary Medgar Evers and called for justice. During the trial that followed, Dr. Howard offered up his home as a headquarters for journalists and Till advocates. To combat the near constant threat of violence, he stocked his house with enough firepower to hold off any possible assault. Howard's pragmatism about violence was not unlike that of Edward Sr. and Scott, whose affable natures were backed by a Winchester in the backseat and a hammer under the front. Even Dr. Martin Luther

King Jr.'s nonviolence was co-signed by the firearms of his comrades (King himself applied for a handgun permit in 1956 after his house was bombed).

Dr. Howard practiced his activism from within the system, through courts and free speech and healthcare. While better-known activists and leaders were making strides on the national stage, Dr. Howard worked in his immediate community. Scott called him their "king of the civil rights movement" for his contributions. Dr. Howard strolled confidently down the halls of power and parlayed with legislators like Theodore Bilbo, the segregationist senator from Mississippi. His speeches about the Till injustice roused other movement-makers like Rosa Parks, who sat in his audience just days before her role in the bus boycott. When she refused to give up her seat in Montgomery, she was still thinking of Emmett Till.[19]

Scott knew Howard as a historical figure, but he also knew him as a man and a doctor. "Dr. Howard did my tonsils," recalled Scott.

While he told this story to his grandson Daniel, Scott pointed to his side, touched his fingers to his stomach, and referenced his tonsils again. "I got some kind of operating tube laying in my side right now where he cut my tonsils out."

Daniel corrected him. "That is not where he cut you at to get your tonsils. They go in through the mouth."

Scott, from his wheelchair, persisted.

"Oh, okay. Alright," Daniel relented. Scott meant to say his appendix. Something else he has survived without. Scott sensed the skepticism. "Yeah, appendix," he agreed at last.

During the time Scott was farming in Mound Bayou, he started seeing stickers plastered to light poles and bumpers in the area telling people, "Don't buy gas if you can't use the restroom." Segregated restrooms and water fountains were constant reminders of the inequity. This message was Dr. Howard's, urging the black community to recognize their power as consumers in the majority-minority Delta. The message Scott received: don't let anybody else tell you where and how to do your business.

19 CANNED AND JELLIED AND FROZEN AND FRIED

Growing up on the farm in the 1950s and '60s was hard work. Scott's seven children were born in the years between 1944 and 1960. The oldest, Felisha Claudette, died when she was four. After Felisha came Rose, Isaac, Vivian, Edward III, Willena, and Octavia. While Scott and his farmhands did the heavy lifting in the fields, the children and their cousins cleaned the house, chopped cotton, and kept the animals fed and watered. Edna Scott fueled it all with her cooking.

Willena Scott-White, Scott's daughter born in 1952, woke up every morning at dawn as a child. "We had to leave the house clean before school. The bus left at about six-thirty in the morning," she said. At the end of the school day she "came home, got off that bus, and went into the field—whatever it was to do. And then came in, got homework, ate supper, . . . went to bed, and got up the next and did the same thing." On summer mornings, when school was out, she and her siblings would go straight into the field.[20]

Isaac Daniel Scott Sr. was the oldest son, and like his father and grandfather before him, he took to the land with a passion. He didn't go to the side fields to chop cotton with the children after school; he climbed on the tractor and helped the men. "I used to get as much done as I could in the day," Isaac said. He was exceptional at cutting the grass on the ditch banks of the rice fields with a curved Kaiser blade. "I could cut just as good as any man out there and was just a child."[21]

The children worked in the fields closest to the house. The land was their babysitter; it kept them in sight from the stoop. In their free time, the children played with the cows and the chickens and the hogs. The favorite spot for Willena and her siblings and cousins was way up high in the loft of the big red barn. There, they invented worlds of loner cowboys and Indian princesses. They went into town only to see the occasional movie or to buy something they couldn't make at home. Edna, who taught herself to make undergarments as a child by studying the pictures in the Sears, Roebuck catalog, hand-stitched everything. Willena remembered going to town in seventh grade to buy a winter coat. It had a raccoon collar. She thought she would love that store-bought coat, but it didn't fit as well as the one her mother made.

The children learned about anatomy, ecology, and environmental science from the yard and the fields and the autumnal slaughter. The Scotts kept the storeroom fully stocked all year long. When it was time to get ready for winter, everyone came up to the Big House where Edward Sr. lived. If they were putting up corn, they'd put up corn for two weeks—enough for everybody on the place. In addition to the crops in the field destined for market, the family tended vast gardens with vegetables of every kind. Summer and fall they jarred and preserved. Scott traveled to Arkansas and brought back loads of peaches, which they made into jelly or cut up and froze.

Chickens ran frantically underfoot everywhere like they had some place or other to be. The women snatched up the birds as they passed and wrung their necks. They let a stunned chicken loose to *jump jump jump* until it keeled over dead. After that it entered the production line.

"You had one crew whose job was to put him in hot water, and then it went on to the next crew and they plucked the feathers off," recounted Willena. "And then cut him up. They didn't throw anything away. From the chicken feet to the chicken butt; they had something to do with all of it."

In autumn the adults gathered in the yard to kill the pigs. They slit their throats with Buck knives, drained the blood, and boiled off the hair in a big pot. One group rendered pork skins in a giant skillet for cracklins. Another team boiled chitterlings in an open-air cauldron. The children on the periphery of the killing heard the squealing of the pigs and the shrill clucks of the fowl, the bubbling fat and boiling water.

This was Edna's world. She embraced the role of keeping the families clothed and fed. The calculations and pantry lists she made on Sundays in the margins of the crossword governed how many, what kind, and in what order. Her storeroom was meticulously kept and encyclopedic in scope. Security for months of barren winter. Everything once living found new life—and gave life—in Edna's kitchen.

20 I'M GOING TO FARM

Juanita, Scott's mother, inherited the estate when Edward Sr. passed in 1957. Before she died in 1970, Scott's sisters convinced their mother that Scott already had plenty of land and wouldn't object to the property being distributed among the other sons and daughters and farmed as one, as it always had been. But for the most part, the siblings did not want to farm. They wanted to sell. Scott scrambled to keep the land together.

He bought up what he could, but much of it was sold outside the family. Alex's hog farm that bordered Scott's land remained in working order until Scott bought it from his brother in 1981. That was the land he would use to farm catfish. His next big acquisition would be family land of a different variety: extended-family land. Isaac Daniel's land in Mound Bayou, to be exact.

Isaac Daniel was facing immediate foreclosure in the late 1970s and had no way to pay his land notes. He owed more money on the land than it was worth. Years of subpar yields and bad money management had contributed to this financial doom. In 1978 Scott bought all 510 acres at a significant markup that rescued his father-in-law from ruin. He paid enough to clear the debt to the banks and then some. As he lay dying in 1981, Isaac Daniel told Scott he'd help him pay the land notes, but Scott knew this was just wishful thinking. He considered the price an investment in the future and in himself. When Isaac Daniel passed, the family lost the last of the sharecroppers-turned-landowners. Scott, now the patriarch, owned 945 acres in 2 counties. His son Isaac owned another 398 acres. Scott leased additional tracts, bringing his operating acreage into the thousands.

The 1970s were high times for row cropping. Scott tied up the highway with a procession of tractors, combines, and bulldozers between his rice and cotton fields in Bolivar and Leflore Counties. "It looked like a parade when we were farming," Scott recalled. He'd drive his equipment over to Mound Bayou for a few days, do what needed to be done, and then move it back home to work on things there. Other drivers had to slow to a crawl behind the Scotts until they could hit the gas and slingshot ahead of the convoy.

"What in the world are you going to do with all that stuff, Ed?" locals yelled up at him as they passed.

The answer was always the same. Scott's mantra: *I'm going to farm.*

Edward Scott Sr. and Juanita Scott at the freezer.
Courtesy of Willena Scott-White.

Cotton field outside Drew, Mississippi. Courtesy of Willena Scott-White.

Barn at Edward Sr.'s "Big House." Courtesy of Willena Scott-White.

Edward Sr. on the farm. Courtesy of Willena Scott-White.

Scott farm and Chevy. Courtesy of Willena Scott-White.

Edna Ruth Daniel
(Edna Scott), age 15.
Courtesy of
Willena Scott-White.

Ed Scott Jr. and Studebaker.
Courtesy of Willena Scott-White.

Ed Scott and his
family. Courtesy
of Willena
Scott-White.

Right to left: Isaac Daniel; Edward Scott Sr.; Dr. T. R. M. Howard; attorney Thurgood Marshall. Courtesy of Willena Scott-White.

Black co-op harvests sixth crop

By DAVID SALTZ
DD-T Staff Writer

RULEVILLE—The Leflore-Bolivar Land Corporation is the largest black-owned business dedicated to agriculture in the United States Saturday, it celebrated its seventh year of existence.

At its annual rice cutting and field day harvest, six miles northeast of here, the corporate owners showed 200 visitors what it takes to start and stay in business.

"Planning and financing are the hardest part," said LBLC President Ed Scott Jr., a rugged 35-year-old Glendora native.

[Ed Scott Jr.]

"The first thing it takes is land you can make a crop on. Then you need equipment. Then good labor. After that, plant the crops you can make good money on," Scott said.

"For example, we stopped planting cotton four years ago. It costs too much and the yields weren't what I would have wanted. This year we planted 1,100 acres of rice and 3,600 acres of soybeans," he said as drivers of five combines harvested a nearby field. Scott predicted a 147 bushel per acre yield, seven bushels more than the previous five-year

represents a better form of crop management.

The land corporation, once called the Leflore County Land Co-op, formally incorporated early this year and gained financial backing to increase the land it owns from 370 acres to 880 acres.

Scott and his sons currently own the controlling interest in the venture that began as a co-op farmed in 1971 by 15 black Leflore County landowners. By pooling their resources and talents, they have helped curb the decline of black-owned land in the rural South.

At the ceremony held in a mammoth tractor shed, Scott presented awards to six men who helped organize the co-op and transform it into the land corporation: H.W. Holliday, president of the Bank of Ruleville, for financial support; Johnny McWilliams, an Indianola attorney, for work in securing a $1,000,000 Farmers' Home Administration loan; F.J. Townsend, a Drew attorney, for helping secure the first 360 acres of land the co-op bought; Charles Bannerman of Greenville, president of Delta Foundation, Inc., for financing the only black-owned rice storage facilities in Mississippi; Vance Nimrod of Greenville, manager of technical services and special projects for Delta Foundation, for technical assistance during the last 5½ years; and Isaac Scott, Ed Scott Jr.'s son and general manager of the farm, for loyal service to the operation during its first six years.

Scott said the corporation, which farms land here and near Mound Bayou in Bolivar County, employs 12 full-time laborers. It hires another 15-20 workers to help harvest beans and rice, a 12-hour-a-day project that lasts 6 weeks.

I.D. Thompson, a former Bolivar County Agent, told the gathering that the land corporation "shows what can be done when technology and

Cooperative Development Fund, which helped the co-op get off the ground with a loan for operating capital and machinery, made a plug for black capitalism.

"It's not good enough for blacks just

Greenville's newly appointed city prosecutor, briefly addressed the gathering.

K. Shalona Morgan, director of public affairs for Mississippi Action for Community Education, Inc.

Staff photo by Ed Saltz

James 'Son' Thomas of Leland sings and plays the blues

Rice Festival, *Delta-Democrat Times*, September 24, 1978.

SCENES FROM 3RD ANNUAL RICE FESTIVAL

(See related story on page 7) Photos By Ruthie Fulton

Sarah Johnson, Greenville Councilwoman, enjoys a cup of RC.

In the rice field.

James "Son" Thomas (right) sings blues as his son accompanies him on guitar.

Bill Wallace sings the blues with Frost Trio.

Kids enjoy rice shower.

Kids and grown ups load up in auger for a joy ride to the rice fields.

Rice Festival, *The Voice of SHIMPH*, October 1977. Mississippi Action for Community Education Inc. (MACE), Mable Starks, CEO.

Digging the ponds. Courtesy of
Willena Scott-White.

Children in the fields. Courtesy of
Willena Scott-White.

Children in the fields. Courtesy of Willena Scott-White.

Ed Scott, happy.
Courtesy of Willena
Scott-White.

Ed Scott's catfish-processing plant. Courtesy of Willena Scott-White.

Ed Scott speaking at plant opening.
Courtesy of Willena Scott-White.

Ed Scott at plant opening.
Courtesy of Willena Scott-White.

Plant ribbon cutting. Courtesy of Willena Scott-White.

Isaac Scott. Courtesy of Willena Scott-White.

Edna Scott at the plant opening. Courtesy of Willena Scott-White.

Edna Scott's cafeteria. Courtesy of Willena Scott-White.

Inside Edna Scott's cafeteria. Courtesy of Willena Scott-White.

Plant workers (left to right): Sophornia Carr, Viola Carr, Lillie Watson-Price, Diane "Shug" Byest, Willie Mae Curry. Courtesy of Willena Scott-White.

Eva Brooks (left) and Elnora Mullins (right).
Courtesy of Willena Scott-White.

Lillie Watson-Price in the plant office. Courtesy of Willena Scott-White.

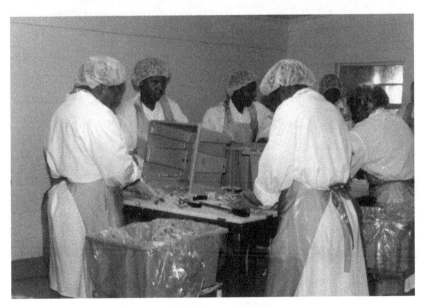

Processing catfish. Courtesy of Willena Scott-White.

Ed and Isaac Scott frying fish.
Courtesy of Willena Scott-White.

Plant in decay, 2013. Courtesy of
the author.

Plant site, 2013. Courtesy of the author.

Tour of the ruins with Daniel Scott. Courtesy of the author.

What remains of the front door to the plant office. Courtesy of the author.

PART II STALK

21 CHOICE

Ed Scott dreamed deeply of his past. Sometimes he was a boy again. Or back in the ditch with Patton. Most often he just relived his day on the farm, the sticky heat stickier in his vivid dream world, the sky blinding blue, the dirt radioactive orange. Scott dreamed of real life because every day he lived his dreams. He made the choice early on to be a farmer, to forgo his classroom education for one in the field. He enlisted to fight in World War II because he wanted to stand and be counted. But Scott wanted his children to be able to make different choices. In the Delta, though, some choices weren't always a choice.

The public education system in the Delta didn't invest in black children. Jim Crow segregation had long prioritized white students over their minority counterparts. When faced with federal mandates, most southern localities did not comply. Ten years after the landmark *Brown v. Board of Education* ruling in 1954 rejected "separate but equal," only about 2 percent of black students in the Deep South attended integrated schools.[1] Gerrymandered districts, whites-only private schools, and a campaign of intimidation excluded black students from quality education. Their underserved districts and deteriorating facilities remained unchanged.

The Civil Rights Act of 1964 set the stage for real reform. It included "freedom of choice" provisions that allowed students and their families to choose which school in the area to attend. Whites could no longer self-segregate their schools by the mere geography of their residences. Even with the federal law backing them up, black families felt intense pressure from the white community to stay put. Relatively few black families sent their children to the better-off white schools. The Scotts were an exception.

Willena Scott-White was in ninth grade when her father moved the family from nearly all-black Mound Bayou—where they'd been living and working on Isaac Daniel's old land—back to Leflore County. Leflore County had more white families than Mound Bayou. In the arithmetic of the Delta, more white students meant better schools with better funding. Scott and Edna discussed the move, then sat down with their children before making a final decision. Scott told them that a good education was the one thing that could take you anywhere you wanted to go. He also told them that entering the white Leflore County schools wouldn't be pleasant. Willena and her siblings said they understood.

"To me, education is power," Willena said. "When you can . . . do better just because you've learned. . . . That's just in us. If there's something you need to do, you learn how to do it right."

It wasn't until middle school in the early '60s that Willena understood that school was for genuine learning. Nothing about her falling-in red schoolhouse in Mound Bayou had emanated scholarship. It was a crumbling façade with hand-me-down history books that, during the Kennedy administration, still ended at Eisenhower. Students were told not to climb the slanted stairs to the second floor because the boards and beams were rotten. "School was just something you went to," remembered Willena. It wasn't about learning. Many rural black students were in class for only three to six months out of the year, Willena said, dictated by the harvest and planting seasons.

In Mound Bayou, there was no opportunity for black students to choose better schools. Because of its proud history of black self-determination, the town had no demographic diversity. There were none of the institutionalized benefits of a white tax base that more mixed districts had. The small Mound Bayou district was governed by a black superintendent who answered to the county school board. The white administrators—mostly wealthy businessmen—allocated funds for books, building improvements, and operating budgets. Not unlike black farmers, superintendents of black districts had to plead with the white higher-ups for resources. James Baldwin writes that they "trudged down back lanes and entered back doors, saying 'Yes, sir' and 'No, Ma'am' in order to acquire a new roof for the schoolhouse, new books, a new chemistry lab. . . . They did not like saying 'Yes, sir' and 'No, Ma'am,' but the country was in no hurry to educate Negroes, these black men and women knew the job had to be done, and they put their pride in their pockets in order to do it."[2]

When the Mound Bayou school district *could* find money for books or curtains or a coat of paint, the money sometimes came not from the school system but from the toil of the students themselves. To combat underfunding, students spent some of their class time each year working as day laborers to raise money for the district. They came into class for roll call, then boarded buses and rode out into the country to chop cotton at a discount for one of the local plantation owners. The plantation owner prided himself on being a generous benefactor to a black school system that was atrophied precisely because of vested white bosses and prone black laborers. These fundraisers were the most literal of school field trips—into the field.

Willena didn't understand the disparity until she started eleventh grade at the high school in Itta Bena, about a half-hour drive from the Leflore County farm. On the first day of school, overwhelmed by the newness and the whiteness, Willena ducked into the bathroom. She stared at the shiny, clean tiles and the functional plumbing and realized, then as never before, how second-rate her past schools had been. In Itta Bena, the teacher-to-student ratio was a healthy one-to-eighteen. There was room to breathe. Back at Mound Bayou she'd shared biology class with sixty-three other students and not enough books to go around. Her assigned seat had been on top of the heater near the window.

Willena and her sister were the only black students on the Itta Bena bus. The bus driver was a shaky old man who was scared to pick them up on the roadside because they were black. Two children of a local white farmer weren't allowed to ride with the Scotts, so the father drove them in the pickup every morning, following right behind the yellow school bus. Willena, watching through the back window of the bus, saw the shotgun lying across his dash. It was a fixture, as sure as the air freshener that dangled from the mirror. Willena didn't fear that shotgun anymore. She remembered what her elders would say about copperhead snakes in the woodpile: he's more afraid of you than you are of him.

The county buses from all the rural feeder routes met at the white Sunnyside Elementary School, where the younger children got off and the high school students consolidated into just a few buses for the final leg. The man in the pickup truck let his children out there, and they ended up on the same bus as the Scott girls after all. For all his hatred of blacks, Willena imagined the man just didn't have enough gas money to make the trip all the way to Itta Bena every morning.

22 EDNA

Edna Scott was much quieter than her husband. When she did speak, people bent to listen. She made sure Willena and the girls took music lessons and were exposed to art and culture. In the bathroom at the house, her children recalled, she always had a set of *Child Life* magazines, a Bible, and a prayer book. You always had something productive to read.

Being home for her children was important to Edna. "Because I had four girls I wanted to stay at home," she said, "and not have my children have to go to school and come home by themselves."[3]

So Edna was a beautician. She did hair right there in the house. She was a cook. She sold cakes baked in her reliable Chambers range. She was a seamstress. She tailored so many garments that carpal tunnel syndrome and arthritis deformed her fingers.

"My hands are gone but I'm not complaining," said Edna. "Everybody don't raise their children, you see. They let them grow up, but they don't guide them to what life is about. The first lesson a child can get is to see what mama and daddy is doing."

23 JOINING THE MARCH

In 1965 Scott made the trip to Selma, Alabama, loaded down with supplies. He came to feed the activists, as he would do at times throughout the 1960s, but he also came to march.

On Sunday, March 7, hundreds of participants set out from Selma, bound for Montgomery, the state capital. The previous month, in February, a state trooper had shot and killed activist and deacon Jimmie Lee Jackson in nearby Marion, Alabama, during a peaceful protest. SCLC's James Bevel and other leaders recommended a dramatic march as a cathartic response. The original plan was to deliver Jackson's body to the steps of the state capitol as a symbol of public outrage. It morphed into a broader demand for equal representation in the state's and nation's political process.

Six hundred marchers attempted to cross the Edmund Pettus Bridge outside Selma on that "Bloody Sunday." State troopers stood waiting on the other side. As the marchers crossed, troopers in gas masks beat them with blackjacks and sprayed tear gas into the crowd. Lawmen rode through the crowd on horseback like Confederate cavalry. They beat the marchers off the bridge and back into adjacent neighborhoods as television cameras looked on. Footage of the conflict fueled public outcry, pressuring the federal government to intervene.

Dr. Martin Luther King Jr., who had traveled to Selma in the wake of Deacon Jackson's murder, organized a second attempted crossing on March 9.[4] Governor George Wallace refused to provide security, and the marchers were overwhelmed and turned back a second time. As they were waiting for reinforcements, Scott—who had watched the clashes on television at home—pulled into town. It was the morning of March 21.

The heavy military presence gave Scott flashbacks to basic training. President Johnson had dispatched more than a thousand U.S. soldiers to watch over a third attempt to cross the bridge. Other men in black suits, Scott learned, were FBI. He drove past jeeps and transports of the Alabama National Guard, called in as part of the protective detail. They wore helmets and shouldered machine guns. The National Guard corralled the local and state police, who had inflicted the initial violence, in a parking lot away from the action.

Scott joined a mass of marchers at a church. There wasn't enough room in the chapel to hold them all, so they lingered outside below a loudspeaker. The crowd buzzed—Dr. King was about to speak. "We didn't know when [King] got there," Scott said. "Nobody knew where

he came from or nothing. All they knew was that they heard his voice."
King's voice came over a loudspeaker, crackling at first, then with great
clarity. His words echoed the sentiments of earlier speeches—they'd all
come too far to turn back.

Marchers gathered at the bridge. Spiritual refrains rang as the peaceful mob locked arms. Where they had clung to a narrow sidewalk along
the edge of the bridge on previous attempts, they now moved freely in
the roadway, protected by President Johnson's reinforcements.

Scott heard marching songs roll up and down the line. The marchers
walked upright on the very spots where they'd earlier been dropped and
bloodied. This time, nothing could block their way. They had five days
and fifty-four miles ahead. Some who could not make it to the termi-
nus walked in solidarity across the bridge. Scott stepped back onto solid
ground and kept walking. He cackled, "If you're going home, you better
get off now! You don't, you'll end up in Montgomery!"

24 THINGS FIXING TO CHANGE

The Scott children made bologna sandwiches for hours, stacking them
on the table like brickmasons building a wall. When they were through,
Edna put them in a cooler to keep them fresh. Scott carried the cooler
outside to the truck and put it in back with the water jugs and Cokes. It
was June 1966.

Across the Delta, word of the march had spread. James Meredith had
become famous in 1962 as the first African American student to successfully enroll at the University of Mississippi. His presence sparked riots.
By 1966 he was a law student at Columbia University. Still carrying the
standard, he conceived of a two-hundred-mile walk from Memphis to the
Mississippi state capital of Jackson. Meredith called it the March against
Fear. The purpose of the march was to inspire voter registration, to defy
the southern politicians and white leaders who intimidated and discouraged black voters from exercising their civic power. On day two of his
journey, June 6, a local hardware store clerk near Hernando, Mississippi,

ambushed Meredith with a shotgun blast and left him bleeding on the side of Highway 51. He was rushed to the hospital. As Meredith recuperated, activists from the Student Nonviolent Coordinating Committee (SNCC), the Southern Christian Leadership Conference (SCLC), and other civil rights organizations expanded the ranks and resumed the march to Jackson. Meredith would rejoin the march about three weeks after his shooting. By then the march was fifteen thousand strong.[5]

The route snaked through the Delta towns of Greenwood, Indianola, and Belzoni. Young children weren't quite sure what it all meant. A friend of the Scotts, Harvey Green (who grew up to become the mayor of the little town of Renova, where Willena Scott-White now lives), remembered his mother being worried when the march came close to home. She called her husband at work and told him to come straight to the house. Harvey and his siblings asked what was going on. All his mother would tell them was "things fixing to change."[6]

Scott knew that the marchers who walked ten miles each day would be tired and hungry. He slammed the tailgate shut and told his family he'd be back soon enough. Scott drove in quiet, kept company by his stalwart hammer under the front seat. It was midafternoon by then. The marchers were out on the open road and scheduled to stop for the night near Belzoni.

The marchers included farmers in cowboy hats and students in cotton shirts. Most were black. In Greenwood, black community leaders promised them an elementary schoolyard as a campsite, but when they arrived, local white officials turned them away. On this evening, when the group got to Tchula, right outside Belzoni, they stopped at a black church. Scott had caught up with them a few miles back and followed, coasting slowly. The marchers thought the church would be a good place to rest before walking into Belzoni for the night. But the preacher saw them coming. Afraid of trouble, he locked himself inside the sanctuary.

Marchers knocked repeatedly on the doors, asking him to give them something to drink. Scott, by the roadside, watched. When he saw that the preacher wasn't opening up, he hollered over, "Come on, I got some water on the truck you can get!"

After they rested, the marchers continued to Belzoni. They camped at a more welcoming church. Scott unpacked and spread the meals out on tables. It was nothing but bologna on white bread, but the marchers ate hungrily.

The sun dipped below the trees in the churchyard, and for a moment the tension waned. A white policeman kept watch. Not *over* them but *on* them. During dinner, the cop walked over. "All y'all out here eating that food over here," he yelled into the crowd, "I don't want to see nothing left on the ground. Nothing!"

Night fell and Scott packed up to leave. The cop's door closed after Scott's like an echo. Scott started back up the highway. The policeman got behind him and followed him north. Down dark stretches of highway the policeman followed. Scott hadn't asked for an escort. Past the congealed swampland, his headlights ever steady. Scott focused on keeping his truck between the lines. "They wanted to see if I'd do something illegal so they could arrest me—maybe kill me," Scott said. "But I didn't do nothing. Kept my speed all the way home."

Scott packed his truck like that many times. He followed the news about Dr. King and others and met them along the way. The prospect of food resonated in sit-ins across the South when activists demanded a shared meal at a shared countertop. Families talked about the movement over dinner. And because every man and woman must eat, food was a common symbol of humanity. The fellowship that Scott offered from his truck bed galvanized the revolutionaries and bolstered their appetites for change.

25 SHARECROPPER'S SON

Scott didn't believe in excuses. If the cotton didn't grow, it was an opportunity to learn and do better. When grocery money was tight, you pulled food from the garden. Scott saw this enterprising mindset at work in nearby Ruleville, where his neighbor, civil rights heroine Fannie Lou Hamer, lived and farmed.

Fannie Lou Hamer was strong, physically and spiritually. She was born the youngest of twenty children in 1917. The shoes and the clothes and the biscuits went to her bigger brothers and sisters, leaving her wanting. This upbringing informed her understanding of food as a symbol of disparity. After being refused service at a roadside café, Hamer was unjustly arrested, jailed, and severely beaten.[7] She emerged from that experience and her sharecropper beginnings to become a leader in voter registration efforts in the Delta in the 1960s while assisting SNCC.

Charles McLaurin, a young student-activist in the Delta at the time, said Hamer was their "shining example." She modeled, in everything she did, the power of the people. When McLaurin became a father himself, he remembered Hamer's hunger. "In my house," he said, " . . . my rule was that the little fellas ate even if the big ones could not. . . . If there are ten biscuits, the little fellas get theirs first. . . . The little fella has got to eat."[8]

Hamer walked onto plantations to register black sharecroppers. "They were picking cotton and she went down to register them," Scott said. "White man on the farm wanted to know who she was. Somebody told him that she was there to register people. 'Register what?!' the white man said. 'Ain't no niggers gon' register around here.' And that was the wrong thing to say to her. . . . She started from then on doing what she wanted to do like she wanted to do it."

Hamer shook up the 1964 Democratic Convention in Atlantic City, testifying before the party's credentials committee and the television media about why she believed the largely African American Mississippi Freedom Democratic Party should have more power in the political process. She recounted her own brutal abuse and put a face on the civil rights crisis that politicians so often addressed with gloved generality. Democratic presidential nominee Lyndon Johnson, who hoped to avoid public controversy during a contested campaign, called a desperate press conference following Hamer's remarks to redirect media attention from her biting truth.[9]

For years, Hamer lived in Ruleville near the Scotts. In the early 1970s she formed the Freedom Farm Cooperative as a cooperative endeavor that gave other former sharecroppers a new and productive start. They built homes and grew food and raised hogs. Hamer even started the Pig Bank, which loaned out pregnant gilts to needy households. The interest, in the form of baby pigs, was shared between the bank and the family. "Families cannot live on vegetables alone," Hamer is quoted as saying. She saw Freedom Farm as a utopia where labor and food and opportunity were given equitably. Where new things could be made from troubled history. On their first forty acres, members of the co-op planted beans, greens, corn, sweet potatoes, and "just enough cotton to keep old memories alive."[10]

Freedom Farm wasn't making enough money, though, so after a difficult year, Hamer came to Scott and asked for help. Scott's blunt diagnosis was that some of the men she had working as farmhands didn't know a thing about farming; Scott freely shared with Hamer the knowledge that his father had passed to him. But advice alone couldn't save the venture. The Freedom Farm experiment succumbed to the capitalist realities of southern agriculture. Fannie Lou Hamer died in 1977 before she could revive it.

In Fannie Lou Hamer and Dr. T. R. M. Howard, Scott saw two complementary examples of African Americans effecting change. Dr. Howard was a believer in entrepreneurial self-improvement in the tradition of Booker T. Washington and an embodiment of the black intelligentsia. Fannie Lou Hamer was a hard-nosed dreamer forged in the experience of the common man and woman. "Whether you have a PhD. . . or no D, we're in this bag together," she said. "And whether you're from Morehouse or Nohouse, we're still in this bag together." Scott's fantastical notions of building catfish ponds of his own volition complemented Hamer's visionary Freedom Farm, and his role as a business leader reinforced Howard's belief in black power through economics.

"The idea [back then] was black power," reflected Charles McLaurin, sitting outside the Fannie Lou Hamer Memorial Garden in Ruleville. "And we got that now. Basically every county in this Delta has blacks in public office. I even have a black sheriff here and in counties around. What we don't have is economic power. White folks still have all the money. Still run all the banks. All the stores."

Scott was an activist, but he was also a committed capitalist. He had as much in common with America's titans of industry as with its social justice revolutionaries. He believed that competition, individual achievement, and leadership could contribute to the common good. The more money he made in farming, the more workers he could hire in the community. While he participated in the civil rights movement, Scott waged his real fight on the front lawn of entrenched southern agribusiness. He battled them for money and market share, and for his own sense of self-worth as the son of a sharecropper. When they could, the Scotts chose their battles.

26 ISAAC

After Dr. Martin Luther King Jr. was assassinated in Memphis on April 4, 1968, riots broke out across the country. While the largest uprisings were reported in cities such as Washington D.C., New York City, Baltimore, Chicago, and Pittsburgh, the frustration came fiercely to smaller cities across the South. Isaac was in Nashville studying agriculture at Tennessee State University. On the night of the riots, Isaac and his cousin were working their shifts at a gas station near the campus of Fisk University, at the corner of Jefferson Street and what is now Dr. D. B. Todd Jr. Boulevard (named for the first black cardiovascular surgeon to practice in Nashville).[11] As angry mourners filled the streets, his supervisor told Isaac to close up shop in anticipation of what might come. As the masses gathered, so did local law enforcement, reinforced by Tennessee State Troopers and National Guard.[12]

Isaac and his cousin locked up and walked to the car. Isaac felt the city trembling. His cousin turned the ignition, but the engine flooded and stalled. A patrol spotted them and approached. Isaac told them it was engine trouble. A guardsman yelled to "step out of the car!" They stepped out. When Isaac's cousin turned to say something more to the guardsmen, one of them picked him up and slammed him on the hood. Isaac, with his hands behind his back, watched. Another guard got into the car and tried to start it himself. The engine flooded again. "Get back in the car," the guardsman told Isaac, exiting the vehicle. "As soon as that car cranks, get on out of here."

Things escalated that night in north Nashville. Cars were flipped and fires smoldered and people got hurt. "We just wanted to see what was going to happen," Isaac says of the night. "But as soon as that car cranked, we got out of there. I wasn't ready to go to jail."

Scott taught Isaac what it took to resist the tides of oppression in America: an education, an applied skill, and a little faith in oneself. When the Army drafted Isaac in 1970, he tested his father's philosophies in the forests of Vietnam.

Isaac was stationed at Long Binh Jail (known at LBJ) in Dong Nai Province, South Vietnam. He honed his mechanical skills on his job as a rough-terrain machine operator; helicopters dropped him into isolated patches of jungle where he cleared the land for Army infrastructure with a bulldozer while gunfire rang out upriver. Isaac liked the job. He was good at it. He didn't expect his supervisors to try to take it away.

But one day, Isaac's commander called him in and asked if he'd trade places with another soldier, a well-connected white guy from New York. This white soldier didn't like his current posting, the dangerous job of combat engineer (they went in ahead of the bulldozers to sweep for mines). Using the guile of Br'er Rabbit, the officer flattered Isaac, told him that he would make a great combat engineer. Isaac was strong, the officer said. He had more guts than the other man, the kind of courage that thrives in war. Isaac was to train the new guy and then step aside. But Isaac didn't like the idea of walking blind through the tall grass looking for explosives. He said no. The officer didn't like the answer. He had it in for Isaac for the rest of the tour.

Isaac's second run-in with Army authority came because of a migraine. It was early in the morning. Isaac pulled the covers over his eyes to block out the light. He'd had headaches before, but nothing like this. They came in the early hours and flattened him helpless in the bed. "It's just dehydration," another soldier told him. "Drink some water." But the migraine didn't leave. Isaac stayed in bed and missed formation. He heard the boots of the commander coming in to rouse him; they stopped at the foot of his bed. Isaac didn't risk the light to take a peek. The commander grabbed Isaac by the ankle to pull him out of bed. Isaac kicked reflexively and sent the commander flying two bunks over. Stunned, the commander picked himself up with an angry, disbelieving grin. "I know you must be sick if you're kicking me!" he howled.

Isaac mustered a response. "I don't know who you are and don't care who you are. I need my head to stop hurting."

The commander brushed the wrinkles out of his uniform and turned to leave. "Get this boy to the doctor."

The doctor turned out to be a psychiatrist—a designated B.S. detector there to separate soldiers with real mental health crises from those who invented ailments to get out of battle. He had Isaac pegged as a faker. The psychiatrist listened to Isaac talk about the symptoms for thirty minutes. When Isaac was through, the psychiatrist delivered a stock diagnosis. "Soldier, only thing I see is you got the same headaches I got when I came over here." Nothing more than anxiety, the doctor concluded. Totally understandable.

"Do what?" Isaac questioned.

"You've got the same headaches I got when I came over here," the psychiatrist repeated. Isaac wasn't in search of opiates or a hall pass. He just wanted his head to stop hurting. The doctor didn't know that Isaac never complained of pain, or about his relentless work ethic, which combined the best parts of his father and grandfathers. Isaac looked no different than a thousand other soldiers. The Army trusted him with a loaded .45 and a million dollars' worth of equipment, but not enough to believe him when he said his head hurt. Such was the institutional paternalism that sowed the southern black experience.

"Well, you explain this to me," Isaac said, "and I'll believe what you're saying. Your head is sitting on your shoulders." He pointed. "My head is sitting on my shoulders." He lightly touched his temple. "Now how are they the same headaches?"

Isaac left the psychiatrist with two pills. He took one and it knocked out the headache instantly. He never took the other. When he recovered, Isaac made up for lost time. There was ground to level and there were bases to build out here on the fringes of the world. Isaac needed to work. He knew who he was when he worked.

27 VERTICAL INTEGRATION

In the 1970s Scott lived and died by rice and soybeans. The grain silos on Scott's land where he stored these crops were the tallest structures for miles. They rose like steel tenements from the flat fields, four stories tall. Scott built them out of necessity. Before, he'd relied on the local grain elevators to weigh and dry the crop. But these middlemen charged for that valuable service. They were also known to be creative with their arithmetic; the black farmer was never sure if he was being dealt with fairly. It was watching another farmer get cheated that decided Scott.

Scott had been sitting in the office at the elevator waiting to weigh his crop. The man before him had brought a load of rice that had too much moisture. He asked if the elevator could dry it down. The man in charge told him yes and that they'd give him a call when it was done. After this farmer left, the elevator men weighed the rice. One of them held out the farmer's ticket to the other and shook his head. "We need to settle with him in here, but our ticket's going to pay him too much. Make up a ticket and don't let him see the other ticket."

Scott looked up from his magazine in the corner. He had been sitting so still, maybe they'd forgotten he was there. *Ain't this a trip*, Scott thought. *Stealing that man's rice right here in front of my face.* After a while, the elevator man called Scott's number. Scott took the ticket. He looked the man in the eye to see if he'd break the stare. "I've been bringing my rice here for many years," Scott said. "[But] before I bring any more here, I'll dump it off the Sunflower River bridge if I can't get no grain bin built." And he left.

Isaac had a similar firsthand experience when he took a load of soybeans to the elevator. "Wasn't no vegetation in the field," Isaac said, which meant that there was hardly any chaff to toss away. When the men weighed it, they came back and told Isaac it was 14 percent vegetation and that they'd be subtracting that amount from the payout. Isaac went to four elevators that day until he found an honest operator who gave him the numbers straight: only 3 percent vegetation in the whole load. "My daddy used to have a saying," said Isaac. "You have to make two crops: had to make one for yourself and one for the elevator."

Scott built three grain bins. But when he stood back and looked, they didn't seem like they'd be enough for all the rice he planned to grow. So he put up two more right beside them. He dreamed big. "We filled them up one year to the brim," Scott said. "I'm talking a [coffee] stirrer wouldn't work in there."

28 GAMBLE

Farming is like going to the casino, a veteran farmer once advised. It's a gamble. You don't realize you've lost until you pull the handle and all your money's gone. Scott experienced his share of bad luck, but the pendulum swung favorably, too. In 1978 he made a million dollars in rice.

The 1977 crop had been dried and stored in the grain bins for months. In fall of 1978 Scott loaded it into a half dozen big trucks and sold the whole lot. Just in time to fill the bins back up with another huge harvest.

The Scotts sold their rice to companies like Comet and Uncle Ben. Rice buyers from the corporations came to Mississippi to inspect samples and make bids based on product quality. In these blind inspections the identity and skin color of the farmer were undisclosed, and Scott's crop impressed.

Scott's eight-year-old grandson Daniel perched high on the ladder on the side of the grain bin and watched. Big trucks with big trailers snaked in from the distant highway and cut deliberate turns around the bends in the road. The drivers pulled up to the grain bins, and Scott's farmhands switched on the augers that pumped rice into the trucks through a long, elevated pipe.

Others harvested the drained fields in the combine and on tractors, flinging mud. The combine spun its forward-facing teeth and cut the rice just below the grain heads. Tractors pulling rice buggies bounced alongside and caught the rice. When a full rice buggy peeled off toward the grain bins, an empty one took its place. The combine hummed along and ate and ate. It was Scott's biggest farming triumph to date. Daniel watched his grandfather shake hands with some businessmen by a parked pickup. From the ladder of the grain bin, tractors looked like Tinker Toys. Men were ants. All but Scott. He was a giant in Daniel's eyes.

It was from the precipice of the grain bin and the lap of a friendly pilot flying a crop duster that Daniel saw beyond the confines of the field. You're never more than a few feet above ground level in the Delta, and whether or not people acknowledge it, the vantage point affects them. It's hard to see the horizon line beyond the trees. Hard to know where you're headed. The purview of the y-axis, thin air and rolling valleys, isn't a practical concern for the average Deltan, who's more concerned with the geography of two dimensions. Forward. Back. Side to side. The landscape encourages a certain nearsightedness, a turning inward to community and basic needs and the work at hand. It can be suffocating for those who want out and comforting for those who want to stay. The change in perspective was dramatic for Daniel, as it must have been for expat freedmen gone north after the turn of the century, looking out from the high-rises of Harlem and Chicago and Detroit, and thinking back to their dirt-floor Delta past, where all was flattened.

The Scotts marked the end of the harvest with an annual rice festival. The workers relished this final bit of real labor—emptying and restocking the grain bins. When the last eighteen-wheeler pulled away with last year's harvest, the men nodded to a group of nearby children, who ran and gathered beneath the auger hose, their arms held up to the sky. As they were showered with falling rice—the dregs of the grain bins—they threw handfuls into the air like doubloons. The boys and girls, Daniel Scott among them, hustled over to an empty rice buggy and climbed in the back for a joyride through the fields. They craned their necks and hung their heads over the side of the buggy as they bumped along, watching the bent rice stalks below blur by like a passing current.

The rice festival put the reaping to music. Scott staged the festival in the cavernous tractor shed. Hundreds of folks, neighboring families and fellow farmers, attended the festival. Local politicians ate late-season watermelon and drank cold Nehi. The Staple Singers took the stage—a flatbed trailer—in matching black. They belted out songs like "Freedom Highway" and nearly blew the roof off to the blue Delta sky. The Staples slapped their legs as they sang, and the beat spread through the crowd.

Men took off their hats and hit them against their jeans like tambourines. Children, possessed by sugar, ran in front of the stage and flailed improvised dance steps. Bluesman James "Son" Thomas joined Lil' Bill Wallace on stage, followed by the Delta MACE Aires of Greenville, the Heavenly Gospel Singers of Jackson, the Greenwood Jubilees, and the polished inmate-musicians of the Parchman Band, bussed in from the infamous prison farm. Fall air breezed through. As the afternoon wore on, men went from standing to sitting to laid out on the grass. They had nowhere to be. Time slowed. Scott found a piece of shade and fell asleep in a folding chair, free for a while from obligations to family and legacy and toil.

The jubilee recognized the indivisibility of Delta people and Delta elements. For a black landowner like Scott, it was a celebration not only of that year's achievement but also of the more gradual and continuous progression across the generations toward independence and self-sufficiency. The tradition of the rice festival faded about the same time that changes in agriculture made such harvests harder than ever to pull off. Charles Bannerman, founder of Delta Foundation and president of Mississippi Action for Community Education (MACE), was honored at the festival along with others who helped fund the farming co-op and make Scott's operation possible.[13] That same year, 1978, Bannerman began the long-running and internationally recognized Delta Blues Festival. He'd seen an authenticity at Scott's celebration that he borrowed for his own. At the Delta Blues Festival that next year, Bannerman staged James "Son" Thomas on a flatbed trailer just as Scott had done. "Country people won't come to fancy places," Bannerman said, and "the blues isn't meant for the cocktail circuit." The music emerged out of hard times. Those musicians would manage just fine in a field or a tractor shed.[14]

The rice festival over, the men broke it all down in just a few hours. The cars pulled out and the field was field again. Scott had hit a jackpot with that harvest but had no plans of cashing out. He stood alone in the middle of the levee, as at the apex of a rolling hill. After a minute he stepped down. His mind turned already to next planting season, another valley and another climb. The gamble continued.

29 FIRST AND LAST

The neighbor jerked the wheel and pulled to the side of the dirt road to watch. He got out and stood on the hood to get a better look at Scott, who was standing about a hundred yards away on a bluff of freshly exposed clay in what had only recently been a soybean field. From a distance, it appeared to the neighbor as if Scott was staring into a giant crater where a meteor had landed. Even atop the hood, the neighbor couldn't see what was down there. Scott was looking down at six feet of absent earth that stretched for acres. He envisaged those acres full of water and thrashing catfish. Scott was on the verge of entering history as one of the first—if not the undisputed first—black catfish farmers of his size in the country. The neighbor saw Scott wave his hands and whistle, then he heard an engine roar and saw smoke billow like it was spewing straight from the earth. The illusion only heightened the magic. *Scott is speaking to the ground*, the neighbor thought. *And it's doing as he says.*

Scott had no safety net in this endeavor. If his crops failed, he failed. Having been born on August 27, 1922, he lived through the transition from farming by mule and man to the modern agricultural age of combines, laser-precise machinery, and pvc irrigation. Even with new technologies and massive usda subsidies, well-equipped farmers like Scott had a frighteningly narrow profit margin. Most scraped by on grit and guts and trial-and-error lessons.

With these realities in mind, Scott formed a cooperative in 1971 in the Brooks Farm area of Leflore County. Black farmers shared equipment and pooled their money and labor. More than a dozen farmers joined the co-op, which was incorporated as the Leflore County Area Cooperative (later called the Leflore-Bolivar Land Corporation). The community coalesced around the co-op and around Scott's assets, Scott being the only farmer with access to real capital. The hope was that smaller farmers in the co-op could acquire additional loans and support.

When a neighbor got his small John Deere Model A stuck in the muck of the bayou on the far side of a field one day, other farmers came with their tractors to pull him out. One after the other, they failed. Just when it seemed like the little tractor was stuck for good, from the far side of a nearby field Scott came riding in at the wheel of his massive John Deere Model R—the first diesel tractor John Deere ever built. Without saying a word, Scott hooked a chain to the helpless Model A and ripped it from the mud. *Plop.* Back on dry land. Before riding away, Scott tipped his hat and smiled. "I tell you, . . . just get you a R John Deere tractor and you got you something," he said. The other farmers almost fell over laughing.[15]

At the high-water mark, Scott farmed thousands of acres in Leflore and Bolivar Counties. He was a respected business leader and minority employer who supported a dozen households, including just about anyone from his extended family who wanted to work. Scott was the most ambitious of his peers. Daniel remembered his grandfather flying down the road on payday with a "big ol' knot of money in his front pocket" to pay his workers.

It would be tempting to look at Scott's success in the late 1970s and early 1980s and say that he had it made. He did not. Larger forces dwarfed Scott's fiefdom. Scott's relationship with the lords of agriculture was feudal, demanding obligation and subservience. Despite these constraints, he forged his own path. His vision and execution exposed the inherent fallacy of ordained white supremacy that had long dominated southern agriculture.

Scott faced down the resentment and ill will of the establishment. He weathered institutional discrimination from the highest levels. In the absence of the panthers that had once ruled Delta swamplands, a new threat had emerged in the form of bank presidents and plantation owners and FmHA agency supervisors who manipulated the government cash flow.

FmHA extended credit to the people who were hardest off. Founded in 1946, it emerged out of New Deal policies, programs, and agencies that had supported American agriculture during the Depression. In 1995 the FmHA was renamed the Farm Services Agency.[16] Throughout these reorganizations, the mission has been the same: to provide financial leverage and aid to farmers in rural communities. As traditional agriculture grew more unpredictable and difficult to sustain in the latter half of the twentieth century, government programs subsidized heartland farming. Dollars funded disaster relief in times of flood or drought and bolstered operating reserves. The government provided life support for American agriculture, an important emblem of national vitality, much as it continues to do for Amtrak. Farming is too central an American ethic and ideal and too vital to the collective psyche to let falter.

Owing money to the government was, for farmers, as expected as wearing boots out in the field. But the Scotts had not previously relied on government loans. Until 1978 the Scotts had secured cash directly from community banks, insurance companies, or economic development organizations such as MACE. Scott's father, Edward Sr., had spent the years following the Depression forging connections with bankers and bureaucrats. Scott valued his business relationships at places like the Bank of Ruleville. Until the 1970s he hadn't asked the federal government for money. He didn't think it was a viable option. In some ways, he was right.

Just as FmHA could extend you credit, it could also restructure your loan or even write it off completely. The agency, it seemed to many, treated loans like Monopoly money. It approved, secured, and then subordinated most of the loans to local banks. The banks got their interest on the loan and the surety that came with a government co-signer. Very little cash flowed to farmers through FmHA itself.

Huge sums from FmHA helped sow thousands of acres of farmland and supported countless workers. A $2 billion government investment in 1970 had swelled to more than $15 billion by 1980.[17] But in southern communities with a legacy of segregation and prejudice, the money was not distributed equitably. Scott was sent to the back of the line.

It is difficult to lay blame for the institutional misconduct Scott experienced at the feet of specific individuals. The people who tried to hold him back were pawns of the status quo and employees of a faceless government. As Willena Scott-White put it, "If it hadn't been one man, it would have been another." These men, though, did have names.

30 NEW CHEVROLET

FmHA funded Scott for the first time in January 1978. Vance Nimrod, a white man who worked with Delta Foundation, helped walk Scott through the process. (Delta Foundation aimed to revitalize rural economies and build human capital in disenfranchised minority communities.) On a Thursday morning, Scott met Nimrod by his truck in the parking lot of the FmHA office building in Greenwood. It was a nondescript structure, four brick walls and a roof and little else. It could have housed a small-town dentist's office.

A man greeted Scott and Nimrod inside the door, led them to a table, and left. Another man arrived and sat down across the table. His name was Delbert Edwards, and he was the Leflore County FmHA supervisor. Scott and Nimrod took turns talking, going over the numbers in the loan application. Scott had figured the expenses he'd need for a profitable year of rice and soybeans. Edwards made notes. When he spoke, he talked to Nimrod. In the end, the three men stood up and shook hands. Scott walked out of the office with every penny he'd asked for. *That man didn't even make us sign anything*, Scott thought. *The other farmers were right. It is easier to get your money from the government.*

Scott returned to FmHA the next year. This time he came to the office without Nimrod. Instead, he brought Isaac. Father and son sat down with Edwards at the very same table. Edwards pulled the file from the previous year. He opened it up and laid it out. But Edwards didn't say anything right away. He sat still, waiting. A few long seconds passed as the men looked at each other. As Scott remembered it, Edwards finally asked them, "Where's that other person?"

"What other person you talking about?" said Scott.

"I'm talking about that white man. Where's he?"

"He wasn't part of us," said Scott. "He was just with us to help us get our money."

Edwards looked surprised. His dropped his pen and it bounced on the table. "He wasn't part of y'all," Scott heard Edwards say softly.

Edwards picked up his pen. With it, he began marking through the figures on Scott's loan application.

During the middle of the meeting, the office broke for lunch. Out in the parking lot, the Scotts got into the truck to go grab a bite to eat. As Scott climbed inside the family Chevrolet—always a Chevy—Edwards spoke to him from a few parking spots away. Isaac recalled him saying, "Ed, that a new truck?"

"Yeah," said Scott, leaning his head out of the window.

"Who told you to buy a new truck? Nobody told you to buy no new truck."

"You don't have to tell me to buy a new truck," Scott said, driving off. "I know how to spend my own money."

FmHA officers were not micromanagers by rule. In general, a farmer had the leeway to purchase equipment, feed, irrigation pipes, batteries, work gloves, or groceries as he saw fit. If the farmer was white, it seemed, the agency trusted his financial judgment. "Does your wife need a car this year?" Isaac Scott remembered overhearing an FmHA loan officer ask a farmer. "Let's put a little money in here to get us a car."

That day, Scott got only a fraction of the money he needed. He sat in silence next to his son on the ride home to the farm. He wondered which had been his greatest offense to the white man: the color of his skin, the crease in his pant leg, or the polished paint job on his truck. The black Chevy was like those crisp work suits that Ed Scott Sr. had worn into the fields a generation before: a signifier of respectability that defied hierarchies of master and worker. Scott could have bought an older-model pickup. But he didn't live by the expectations of others. Instead, he bought new Chevrolets. He rode high on his tractor. He spoke truth to power.

31 WHY CATFISH

Scott rose to prominence during a time when demand and price fluctuations for staple row crops like cotton, rice, and soybeans destabilized agriculture. During the mid-twentieth century, farmers profited from a tested range of crops and consistent government-backed subsidies. The primary source of instability was the weather. As U.S. farmers entered world markets, the situation changed.

With globalization, southern crops grew more volatile and farmer demographics shifted. Between 1969 and 1980, the number of individual farms decreased from nearly 1.74 million to about 1 million.[18] At the same time, the size of the average farm increased. Small, independent farmers, white and black, who had been a ubiquitous presence atop their tractors on the Delta roadside, were replaced by large-scale agribusiness. This movement left black farmers buried in the loam. Their ranks had already been declining. Modern restructuring and corporate consolidation exacerbated the slide. In 1950 more than 500,000 black farmers worked land in the South. By 1978 that number had dwindled to about 50,000.[19]

During that same thirty-year period from 1950 to 1980, emerging overseas markets whipsawed between boom and bust. Profits for old standards such as wheat and rice and soybeans oscillated wildly. Agricultural economists predicted more of the same in the years to come. Small farmers suffered the most.

The Russian embargo of 1980 epitomized the uncertainty. In response to the communist superpower's intervention in Afghanistan, President Jimmy Carter cut off all sales of U.S. grain to the USSR, the largest importer of U.S. corn and wheat. The short-lived embargo did little to cripple the USSR, and the American farmer, already walloped by inflation, took the hit when Soviet markets dried up.[20]

How could southern agricultural leaders insulate themselves against these variables to create more sustainable and predictable outcomes? Farmers in the Mississippi Delta looked to a classic southern folk ingredient with big business potential: catfish.

Catfish once occupied the muddy bottom of the American consumer food chain. Long before the fish became a commodity, Southerners hooked cats on cane poles or bought them from enterprising fishermen. Commercial catfish farming was born in Arkansas; farmers were raising fish in the Delta region of that state by the late 1950s. Mississippi followed with its first documented commercial catfish pond in 1965.[21] The alluvial landscape of the Delta proved ideal. The deep soil deposits drained poorly, ready-made for ponds. New technologies and increased industry organization spurred growth. After farmers started to raise the fish, commercial processing plants emerged. Delta Pride in Indianola and Farm

Fresh in Hollandale were two of the first processors in the Mississippi Delta; others included Country Select Catfish in Isola. They cemented the Mississippi Delta as the epicenter of the industry. In 1976 Mississippi governor Cliff Finch proclaimed the Delta's Humphreys County the "Catfish Capital of the World." Belzoni, the county seat, inaugurated the World Catfish Festival that same year. The numbers didn't lie. In 1976, half of the more than fifty thousand acres of catfish ponds in the United States were in a cluster of Mississippi Delta counties.[22] In the decades to come, Mississippi's share of the U. S. catfish production reached 80 percent.[23]

In those early years of commercial catfish farming, farmers marketed their own products, mostly locally. With the formation of catfish trade groups in the state and the emergence of processing cooperatives such as Delta Pride, farmers took advantage of new research, resources, and marketing plans. The Mississippi Department of Agriculture and Commerce helped form the most influential of these trade groups. The Catfish Farmers of America and the Catfish Farmers of Mississippi promised cohesion and organization. Under their leadership, catfish became a bankable commodity. These trade groups introduced new methods for raising, feeding, and processing the fish. Consistency was the goal. With those improvements, farmers could provide a product that appealed to middle-class consumers.

Taste testers graded the fish prior to processing to control against unpleasant flavors. In the industry, a catfish with substandard taste is known as "off-flavor." Off-flavor catfish are the result of environmental factors, including diet, pond contamination, weather, and—most commonly— absorption of bacteria through the skin and gills. Bacteria produced by pond algae are the primary offenders.[24] The fish absorb these bacteria into their fatty flesh, resulting in a medicinal taste. Ever conscious of its brand, the modern catfish industry put in safeguards to remove these off-flavor fish from the market until the pond environment improved.

With a consistent product in place and a network of processors and distributors, industry groups launched informational campaigns and touted the product. During the catfish boom, NBC *Today Show* weatherman Willard Scott sampled the fish on the air, declaring, "If I go down for anything in history, I would like to be known as the person who convinced the American people that catfish is one of the finest eating fishes in the world."[25]

Black farmers like Ed Scott were largely forgotten in this agricultural recalibration, left to figure out their own alternatives to traditional row crops. Delbert Edwards, for example, was utterly surprised to see Scott building his own catfish ponds. He likely assumed Scott's row cropping operation would falter in the wake of declining markets and that would be that. White farmers got together to talk about catfish marketing and best practices, and they didn't talk to Scott. He found out about these networking luncheons thirdhand and attended when he could. Blue plate piled high, he took his seat at a table off to the side. Guest speakers talked about pH levels and irrigation. A sympathetic white farmer once stopped next to Isaac and Scott's table. "I ain't going to let y'all sit by yourself," the farmer said. Scott told him not to worry. He liked having room to spread out. And he didn't mind going it alone.

"I got the sense that FmHA was preaching [catfish] to the group of white farmers and Ed Scott was on the outside of the room listening in," said attorney Phil Fraas, who would become one of Scott's staunchest allies in the future. "[He] wasn't included in that, but he listened well and did it on his own. That, I think, is what really ruffled Delbert Edwards's feathers. [The idea that] that wasn't meant for you, that strategy is not meant for you because you're the black farmer. You're supposed to be the smaller operation and the basic one-tractor-do-your-soybeans-and-that's-it setup."[26]

Though he didn't benefit from inside information, Scott saw the future clearly. He gave himself directives: find funds where you can, become a catfish farmer, dig your own ponds, harvest your own fish, and make your own markets. Do all this—or quit farming.

32 DIGGING IN

"I watched him dig those ponds," said one of Scott's neighbors. "I just woke up one day and they were out there digging catfish ponds. It was absolutely fascinating. And still to this day, it was unbeknownst to me how they did it. All that land, it used to be just rice. And it turned into a fish pond."

Daniel Scott, eleven years old, gripped the wheel of the Case tractor. He had learned to drive his daddy, Isaac's, pickup when he was eight, before he was even strong enough to throw it into low gear, and he'd be working a combine before he was thirteen. Scott had enlisted him to help excavate the ponds. These were giant things, each pond as big as fifteen football fields. Daniel got fancy on the Case and almost flipped the tractor on the incline of the bank. Isaac saved the day, righting the machine with the nose of his heavy-duty pickup as his son teetered on two wheels. Scott and Isaac yelled at the boy, but they didn't tell him to go inside. "It wasn't . . . 'You're thirteen and don't have any business out here anyway,'" recalled Daniel. "It was, 'Now you know better. Get back up there and do this again.'"[27]

Delbert Edwards showed up unannounced just as the Scotts were finishing the last of eight twenty-acre ponds. He didn't drive over to lend engineering advice or to congratulate Scott on his progress. Edwards had gotten wind that a black farmer was digging holes in the ground and calling them fish ponds, and he wanted to see it for himself. He shut his truck door and looked out over the 160 acres of transformed rice fields. Edwards walked toward the ponds. Scott met him halfway. *Now that I have the ponds, maybe me and Edwards could get along after all,* Scott thought. *Now that I can make him some money.* Scott greeted Edwards, who, Scott recalled, had only one thing to tell him: "Don't think I'm giving you any damn money for that dirt you're moving."

No black man had ever bulldozed his way into the exclusive catfish industry like Scott did. He finished his ponds in 1981 and applied for a loan from FmHA for 1982. He needed fish and he needed feed. Edwards was less than enthusiastic. As he ran Scott's numbers for a proposed operating loan, Edwards said little. Scott remembered that while they were discussing how much money FmHA would loan him for fish, Edwards scribbled the figure "50 cents" on the page, presumably indicative of his evaluation of the request. Scott didn't get his money that day.

Scott knew that if he couldn't obtain funding, the ponds would stay empty. With no response from the local office, he made a trip to the state

FmHA headquarters in Jackson. Papers in hand, he pleaded for help to get his money moving. The state arm of FmHA reviewed Scott's situation and told Delbert Edwards to fund the farm. Scott did receive an infusion of cash, but the amount was insufficient to stock all the ponds. He received a third of the approximately $450,000 required to capitalize the operation. Of the eight ponds he dug, he was able to put fish in only four.

33 STOCKING THE POND

The Scotts stood on the edge of the pond wearing galoshes in late summer 1981. Sealed plastic bags full of fingerling channel catfish floated on the surface of the water. Inside the bags, the little fish wriggled in their confined puddles, becoming acclimated. Scott waited and watched. In ten minutes the temperature difference between the water in the bags and the ponds stabilized. Bending down, Scott broke the seal on one of the bags and let the waters mix. The baby catfish, incubated in a climate-controlled hatchery, entered the frontier of the murky water. They swam cautiously from their enclosure into the wider pond, investigating their new surroundings.

Here is Ed Scott's business model for farming catfish in the early 1980s: Scout the land. Dig the ponds and drill the wells. Stock the waters with fingerling catfish bought from a hatchery in the nearby town of Drew. Buy as much feed as possible and launch the soybean-rice-wheat-protein pellets across the pond. Grow the fish to maturity. Harvest the fish. Get them processed, hopefully at the big new processing plant a few counties south. Sell them far and wide.

Scott had done an impressive job of stocking his ponds with some of the money from FmHA. He spent the rest of it on feed, and he needed more. When he went back for more money, Edwards refused. "Let the son of bitches [*sic*] die," he said to Scott.[28]

Catfish begin to reach maturity at around eighteen months. As he managed his first crop of fish, Scott steadily worked to find a processor. The Delta catfish-processing apparatus had developed parallel to the growing industry. Indianola-based Delta Pride was the largest and most technologically advanced plant in the area. Its opening in 1981 helped usher in catfish's modern era. Structured as a farmer-owned cooperative, Delta Pride built relationships with farmer-stockholders who provided a steady supply of catfish, which Delta Pride processed, marketed, and distributed.

To gain entrée, Scott gave the man his family called "Lawyer Townsend" instructions to purchase Delta Pride stock on his behalf. But when P. J. Townsend attempted to make the transaction for Scott, Delta Pride wouldn't sell the stock to him. Townsend relayed the conversation to Scott. He wasn't able to buy Scott stock "according to the color of your skin."

Few farmers had vertically integrated operations of their own. A typical farmer relied on several different companies, services, and funders for his catfish farm to succeed. If Scott couldn't get enough funding, he couldn't buy any more fingerlings or feed. Without a plant to process his fish, he'd be shut out of the marketplace. Scott had planned for this likelihood. He resolved to skin his own fish if it came down to that. Scott didn't get into catfish to wage political war; he wanted to earn a living. When he saw a roadblock, instead of looking for a shortcut, Scott built a new highway. And he barreled down the double-yellow line in his Chevy truck at breakneck speed.

Though he never could buy stock in Delta Pride, the company inadvertently became a resource for Scott. Proud of its state-of-the-art production line, Delta Pride regularly welcomed visitors and potential investors. Scott asked Lawyer Townsend to set up a visit. Townsend's secretary arranged it, telling a Delta Pride secretary that she was sending over two prominent businessmen who would like a guided tour. "If they'd have said two *black men* I probably wouldn't have gotten in there," added Scott. On a clear Delta weekday, Scott and Isaac drove the hour over to Indianola. They were quiet and reflective. "Don't tell them we're here to see what they're doing," Isaac warned his father as they drew close. The complex was imposing and stark against the distant tree line and brushy growth of the surrounding farmland. It was physically large in a part of the state where many homes were small; where big buildings meant big power.

"Don't tell them you're going to process no fish either," he added, "because they aren't going to tell you a thing after that."

"Well," Scott rebutted, "they're just not going to tell me nothing because I ain't going to tell him no lie."

When they arrived, Scott and Isaac sat down in a waiting area. It was forty-five minutes before anyone said a word to them. Both men, participants in the civil rights struggles of the 1960s, were well versed in the proactive tactic of sitting. Finally, a man named Larry came out from the back to say that he would be with them shortly.

Seeing the inner workings of Delta Pride, glimpsing the perpetual motion of man and machine, was like lifting the veil on Willy Wonka's chocolate factory: the hum of refrigerators, the sucking of eviscerators, the RPM drone of head saws, the *zoop zoop zoop* of a hundred blades cutting, cutting, cutting. Plant workers sorted the fish by size and weight, some destined to be packaged filets, others steaks, some sealed and frozen whole. As the fish came down the line, workers deftly severed the bodies from the heads. The next crew snatched the bodies, ripped open the stomachs, and sucked out the entrails. Moving up the line, the skinners took charge. They boxed and labeled the fish, and a different set of gloved and calloused hands in a separate department of the factory stacked them on pallets. This smooth and precise ballet happened almost wordlessly. Black men and women, who filled almost all of the manual labor positions, repeated their calibrated tasks in tandem with the machines.

On the way through the plant, Larry told Scott and Isaac what each person was doing and why. Father and son listened intently. After a while, Larry asked, "So, do y'all have a farm?"

"Yeah," said Scott. He kept walking.

"You got any stock in the plant?"

"Nope," said Scott.

Larry stopped walking. They were near the loading dock now. "You got anything lined up with live haulers?" asked Larry.

"Nope."

"Well, what the hell you going to do with your fish, eat 'em?!"

"Something like that," said Scott. "I'm down here now seeing what you're doing. I'm going to clean my own fish."

34 GROUNDBREAKING

What had been a dirt-floor tractor shed on wooden posts became an insulated, self-contained catfish-processing operation plopped down in the middle of Delta nowhere. Scott financed the processing plant on his own. Frank Brown, a self-taught carpenter from nearby Drew, laid concrete on one side of the plant. Scott paid him half. Brown laid concrete on the other side. Scott paid him the other half. Every little while, he'd call Brown and ask for something new to be constructed. Bit by bit, the plant emerged.

As construction continued at Scott's Fresh Catfish, Scott reached out to Mississippi State University Extension Service's Food and Fiber Center and told a professor there that he was installing a one-line catfish plant. Scott asked him if the center had any literature on it. The man said no, but he'd get something from Auburn University. "Something" turned out to be a four-page pamphlet about what building materials to use inside the plant. No wood, no fiberglass, all stainless steel, it said. That was about all there was to go on. It was all Scott needed to know.

He called the professor and thanked him for the pamphlet. "When I get done," Scott told him, "I want you to come inspect it. When I open the doors, I'm going to be able to sell to anybody." And he did. Scott became an unwelcome catfish dorsal jabbed in the hand of the Leflore County FmHA office. It soon became clear that they wanted this disruptor out of the business for good.

Scott studied the processes of others and kneaded them into his business philosophies. He was as willing to lean on folk methods as on the latest technology. He taught workers to deep-skin the catfish, a little-used technique that yielded a prime cut. The industry now calls a similar cut "delacata." It's considered the best meat on the fish, a sort of catfish tenderloin. Daniel Scott reckons that his grandfather picked up the practice from watching a worker meticulously skin runt fish to take home, a skill that worker might have gotten from his aunt, who got it from her mother, and so on. "Scraping the black stuff off the bellies" is how the Scotts might describe this deep-skinning process to the layperson.

Scott's Fresh Catfish opened on a cold, clear February day in 1983. The air pulsed with excitement. Family, friends, and newly hired plant workers milled in the gravel drive between the plant and the Scotts' home. The one-line plant was smaller than any in the Delta, as far as Scott knew, but it was still larger than the farmhouse where he lived. The builder had expanded the footprint of the tractor shed and constructed a cinder block–walled main killing floor that adjoined the offices and loading dock. Wood-plank siding, laid vertically and painted a bold red, covered the exterior of the administrative wing. The color popped against the adjacent concrete wall, painted white. The finishing touch, hung up just hours before the opening, was a hand-lettered wood panel that said SCOTT'S FRESH CATFISH.

Scott paced, waiting for the right moment to throw open the doors. Jim Buck Ross, the cowboy-hat-and-dark-shades-wearing, no-nonsense commissioner of the Mississippi Department of Agriculture and Commerce, smiled big and shook hands; his warmth defied the temperature outdoors. When it was time, the Scott family and their guests sat down in a row behind the podium. Scott opened his arms to bring the audience closer. In a booming voice he spoke to his friends before him but also past them, as if he were addressing a crowd of thousands. Scott talked of his pride at opening the first black-owned plant processing farm-raised catfish in the nation. Applause and hollering erupted when he cut the white ribbon and invited everyone inside to tour the plant and witness a contest among the line workers to see who could skin the fastest. Initially, workers on the Scott's Fresh line skinned fish by hand. They slit the throat of the fish and hooked it on a nail. With hand-skinners, they clasped the skin beneath the head and shucked it like a wet pair of jeans. Eva Brooks, a driving force inside the plant, out-skinned everybody. Her cousin Darren won the filet contest. There were no prizes, just pride.

After the commemoration, attendees broke apart and talked in small groups. Some went back inside to look around. Others walked around the side of the plant to the concrete vats that would hold the wriggling fish from the ponds. One worker turned on a car radio. When Michael Jackson's "Billie Jean"—released just a month before—came on the radio, the worker cranked the knob as loud as it would go. A group of women plant workers all dressed in black Lee jeans and matching T-shirts picked up the beat and juked across the dirt. The workers pulled Scott and Isaac onto the makeshift dance floor. The two farmers flailed and stomped to the music. Their trademark stoicism had loosened, a bit of oil to the Tin Man's joints. A worker described their movements as "wigging and wopping."

Scott's plant workers were a close-knit bunch. One group of women called themselves "the Dependables." Along with fastest skinner Eva Brooks, this core crew included Lillie Watson-Price, Essie Watson-Maggitt, and Elnora Mullins. They were part of a much larger dedicated team that included the likes of Sophornia and Viola Carr, Diane Byest—known as "Shug"—Willie Mae Curry, and Darryl Scott. The Dependables worked long hours to keep the plant operating. They lived nearby and worked any and all shifts, in snow and storm, amid mud and guts. They were tough. Scott's grandson Daniel, a teenager when the plant opened, called them "mannish ladies." They did everything the men could do, and more. "We packed fish—thirty-pound boxes—and we throwed them boxes just like a man," Eva Brooks recalled. "Those men taking their time, we chucked it like it was nothing."[29]

Many of Scott's workers had been desperate for gainful employment for months or years. Scott gave them jobs and offered them purpose. He trusted and inspired them. Black workers staffed the larger processing plants, too, but there was no dancing there. These minimum-wage employees suffered carpal tunnel from repetitious motion. Others reported sexual assault by their superiors. They were discouraged from unionizing. Women were forced to share communal bathrooms with the men, using stalls that had no doors. Shift managers strictly enforced bathroom break allocations of as little as five minutes a week. Some of these workers opted to wear diapers to avoid the added humiliation of wetting their pants.[30] The Dependables came from the same area and got gas at the same corner store as the workers from other plants. The difference was the particular character of their boss man—their general. Just as Scott had collectively worked the land with his father, without regard for whose name was on the deed, he ran the plant without unnecessary hierarchy. He treated his coworkers with dignity and respect, and it paid dividends. When he was away, the Dependables took charge.

It was as civil rights leader Ella Baker said to young members of the Student Nonviolent Coordinating Committee in the mid-1960s as they left for Mississippi to register black Deltans to vote: "Go and tell the people on the plantations that they don't have to wait on the elite. They don't have to wait on Roy Wilkins. They don't have to wait on James Farmer. They have people among them who are capable of being leaders."[31] Scott's farm grew leaders.

In addition to working the line, answering the phones, and wading in the water, the Dependables cared for their families. They ran home between shifts to fix dinner, help with homework, and draw baths before coming back to the plant to pick up right where they left off. Essie Watson-Maggitt even went into labor at the skinning table. Her water broke mid-fish. She calmly took herself home, drew a bath and soaked, and drove to the hospital, where she gave birth to boy. In a few more tellings, that episode will have become a bit of Delta lore. She will give birth to her son at the skinning table and baptize him in pond water, all the while pulling guts and chopping heads, never breaking her rhythm.

35 BULL MARKET

A week after the plant opened, the Mississippi Department of Agriculture and Commerce (MDAC) put out a press release on official letterhead announcing the first black-owned catfish-processing plant in the nation.[32] Scott broke ground in early December 1982 after seeing the potential for a full-line plant, it read. Even before, in November of that year, he was hand cleaning his fish at home for sale in the Greenville-to-Memphis market. After only two months in operation, the four-thousand-square-foot Leflore-Bolivar plant processed some twenty thousand pounds of catfish per week. Just a few years later they'd be capable of sixty thousand pounds *a day*.[33] Sales reached as far as Detroit. They sold every cut that the big outfits did: whole fish, steaks, filets, strips, nuggets. Wholesale and retail.

You measure catfish in ounces. Two-to-five, five-to-seven, seven-to-nine, and so forth. Scott cleaned the smaller fish and froze them whole. He cut filets and strips out of nine-to-eleven on up to fifteen-to-twenty fish. Anything larger, he sliced perpendicular to the spine into steaks. The nugget sits on the bottom of the fish behind the gills, detached from the filet. He took that, too. "[It] became really popular in the industry," said Daniel Scott. "But wasn't nobody cutting nuggets until he started cutting nuggets."

The workers found even more uses for the fish. They took tweezers to the skeletons and picked off the clinging meat. Out of this mash they made catfish croquettes. They sold inedible refuse to a trucking company that hauled off the guts and skin and the oily nether parts. Lillie Watson-Price had heard that they took it over to Moorhead to make hair cream and makeup and cologne to sell at the 88 Cent Beauty Supply. The truck stunk up the open road; other cars rushed to pass.

Scott and Isaac put their fish in front of and in the mouths of as many buyers as possible, from the big distributors on the East Coast—to whom they shipped hundred-pound boxes gratis—to the midwestern homemaker who had only heard tell of this new-fangled-ugly-mugged channel fish. "We didn't have no problem selling, because our fish were so clean," said Isaac. The deep-skinning process, done by hand to "clean off the black stuff," did give Scott's fish an edge. Even if some of his competitors would later adopt the practice themselves, the workers at Scott's plant believed their care and commitment made their fish better. The same way you might swear that it's your mother's particular love that makes her cobbler so good.

Isaac drove ten hours to Kroger corporate headquarters in Cincinnati, Ohio, in the Scott's Fresh Catfish truck—a retrofitted bread truck—with an iced-down load of his product. After pitching the product to management, he set up inside the grocery store with a table and a fryer and a spider skimmer and started handing out samples. He fried fish the whole afternoon at the end of the cereal aisle and approached every salt-of-the-earth Ohioan he could. They had no idea that the man at the table was one of the operators of the sole black-owned catfish-processing plant in the country.

Most of the shoppers had never tried catfish. Some turned up their noses and kept walking. "I don't want no catfish." A lady and her daughter eyed it. The daughter, feeling brave, snatched a piece and chewed as she walked away. A few minutes later, they lapped back. This time the mother took the plunge. She smiled. "Where'd you find this fish?" she said between chews. Isaac told her the same thing he told everybody else. It came from Mississippi.

From Cincinnati, Isaac drove to Chicago to introduce himself to the fishmongers at the Chicago Fish House, which shipped seafood to establishments in all fifty states. When they saw how clean and white the flesh of his fish was, they went crazy for it, Isaac recalled. He gave them his last box and they placed a small order. A few weeks later, Isaac carried it back up to them personally. The fishmongers cut some of their Delta Pride order so they could buy from Scott.

As demand for Scott's fish eclipsed the supply in his understocked ponds (he could never get enough FmHA financing to realize the promise of 160 underwater acres), he bought fish whole from live haulers and other farmers and processed them for resale. Delta Pride, the family claims, found out about the deal with the Chicago Fish House and pressured live haulers and farmers to cut off Scott's supply. If they sold fish to Scott, the rumor was, Delta Pride wouldn't buy any more from them. Isaac found an anonymous farmer who was willing to sell them enough catfish to fill the Chicago order, but it wasn't enough to continue the contract. Scott and Isaac both made the Windy City drive to deliver the order. They told the Fish House where things stood; there wouldn't be another trip. "But those Chicago guys sure did like that fish," Isaac recalled.

Scott had grand plans for growing the plant's infrastructure and workforce. Agriculture Commissioner Jim Buck Ross, a bright spot in the often-callous establishment, wrote Scott a personal letter offering the department's help if Scott should ever need it. Back at the ribbon cutting Ross had remarked, "An operation with this early success is certainly a credit to our people, creating new employment at a time it is most needed."[34]

"Mr. Scott brought jobs to the Mississippi Delta area," said plant worker Lillie Watson-Price. "I had been in Mississippi three years and I didn't have a job. And we worked really good as a family. . . . We went from food stamps to money!"

PART III REAP

36 HOLD YOUR BREATH

The ponds, partially drained for harvest, trembled. The catfish crowded together, whipping and splashing. The buoys that held up the top of Scott's seine net stretched hundreds of feet across the pond. Weights on the bottom held the net down and kept the fish from swimming under them. The men had unfurled the net on a giant reel. Using tractors on either bank, they pulled the ends of the net across the pond, herding the fish into one rambunctious corner.

Daniel Scott, a scrawny hundred-pound adolescent, stood with his feet on the bottom of the net, where some of the weights had gone missing, while the tractors dragged it through the pond. Scott and Isaac gave Daniel the job of riding the net to see how he fared. "I always wanted to do what they did," said Daniel. "I wasn't complaining about working like a grown man."

He stood firm at first. Daniel felt the tension as the net moved through the water. The catfish grew denser. Daniel felt their bodies against his legs. The pond was six feet at its deepest point. Daniel wasn't nearly that tall. He came closer to the center of the pond, and the water crept up past his belly. Daniel did the math. Then it was at his shoulders. When the net hit the middle, Daniel took a deep breath and let the water envelop him. He closed his eyes and let go into the blackness, shaking water, and panicked fish. He stayed under in the dark, relying on his senses of touch and sound and taste. Scott and Isaac watched from the bank. After a few long seconds Daniel popped up, lungs gasping, and swam furiously to shore. It had been a cryptic lesson from man to boy about the nature of depth in the Delta and the importance of treading water and holding your breath.

When the nets were full and the smaller fish had been given time to wriggle free, the men hoisted the haul into a waiting truck. They off-loaded the fish into vats at the plant where workers stunned the fish with electrified prods before sending them inside for processing.

"I was seeing things that the average person would be way up in life before they got the chance to experience," said Daniel Scott. "Even now, I think a little too big sometimes, because I was used to doing big things."

37 ALWAYS ON CALL

Scott managed his plant differently than the big outfits did. He didn't have a sophisticated human resources department. Working on weekends didn't earn his employees time and a half, and they didn't get paid leave. Scott expected a lot from them, just as he did from himself.

His management style vacillated from exacting to laissez-faire. Sometimes Scott and Isaac walked through the plant monitoring the efficiency and cleanliness of each station like Marine drill sergeants. Other times they'd shuffle through with pockets of ice to hurl like impish schoolboys at the backsides of the workers, who answered in kind.

A rare snowstorm hit the Delta in December 1983 and shut down schools and roads. The plant workers, many of whom drove two-wheel-drive compact cars, were stranded at home. Even the Dependables, after looking outside at the doomsday weather, turned back from their windows, pulled their robes tight, and crawled back into bed—but not for long. Scott rumbled house to house across the ice in his trusty Chevrolet to gather his troops. He'd told them before that no storm would keep them from working. Even when dark clouds pregnant with lightning settled over the plant, the workers stood firm at their stainless-steel stations while thunder shook the shingles.

When he stubbornly tried to work with a bad case of the flu, walking into the office wrapped in a blanket, the Dependables tended to Scott like their sick child. They took him home and visited him later at the hospital when the flu took a turn. Scott didn't show vulnerability to the outside world; only to family. And he trusted his employees as if they shared his name. He recovered in bed and didn't worry about things at the plant. The Dependables made sure everything got done.

38 A LOOK AHEAD

An aging Scott sits in his wheelchair in the middle of the room. It's thirty years since that bout with the flu and he has a blanket over him once again. He listens to the noise from the kitchen, where his daughters Willena and Rose cook. Hot oil pops. Hushpuppies and catfish filets fry. A spaghetti casserole warms in the oven. They make Scott a plate and carry it out to him. Edna sits calmly on a stool at the kitchen island with her hands in her lap and a crossword puzzle on the counter.

Outside, an afternoon thunderstorm moves fast over Renova and the Renova One Stop convenience store on the corner with the town's single stop sign. A strike hits nearby and the lights flicker. Scott, one eye false and the other failing, sits in the shadows and feels around for a filet. He tears off a piece and brings it to his lips. Straight from the fryer, it burns him and he pulls it away.

Somebody knocks at the door. It's the Dependables: Eva, with her sassy smile; Elnora, who moves like a woman in charge; Essie, the little sister of the group; and Lillie, the steadfast secretary of all trades. They haven't all been together or seen their old boss in years. They are already bantering back and forth like they used to, jumping on top of each other's words. They give Scott a big group hug. He grins.

Eva sneaks a bite off Scott's plate. At the plant, she had been the designated flavor checker. You didn't want off-flavor fish on the market with your name on it, and Eva had been the safeguard. She would take a filet and pop it into the microwave for few minutes before savoring the bite like a sommelier. She holds the bite off Scott's plate in her mouth a little longer than normal, caught up in the memory.

"You could tell if it's off-flavor. It's a muddy taste, a sour taste," she says. "If the color 'blue-green' had a taste, that's what it was," she continues. "But this here," she yells into the kitchen, "is good fish."

"I get mad when it's mixed up at Kroger," Lillie comments. Elnora and Essie nod in agreement.

"I takes mine back," Eva continues. "I cook me a good load of it and eat some and then I takes it back." She laughs. "Because some of it's good and some of it's bad—that's just how fish is. I say, 'This fish is off-flavor.

I'm a flavor checker, I did fish for eight years plus. I want my money back.' They give me my money back. They don't want me to start blabbing that to the customer. Because I was a loud talker. 'You don't give me my money I'll tell everybody.'" Not all the processors were as fresh as those women were.

The women sit and hold their plates while they eat. Daniel and Isaac find seats. Edna comes in from the kitchen and sits on the couch. Willena fishes out an old photo album, and the women double over at seeing their younger selves. They'd all had bouncy Jheri curls. Isaac, too. Before they leave, the Dependables gather around Scott a final time. They each give him a peck on the cheek. "Let me tell you something," Scott begins. "I got all my children here. *All* my children. Thank God for this. Thank God for everything. I knowed it was y'all when I first heard *nah! nah! nah! nah!* I knowed it that minute."

39 THEFT

In spring of 1983, just months after the plant opened, Scott experienced the first of a series of foreclosures by various local lenders. Over the course of 1982, FmHA county supervisor Delbert Edwards had made it clear that he was through with Scott. When FmHA refused to fund Scott further, the banks that held the subordinated loans had little choice but to demand the principal; it would have been bad business to continue funding him. As second lien holders, banks that extended money to Scott could get repaid on new loans only after the government got its money. Scott didn't have the cash. He'd turned what he had into catfish. Even though Scott had done the very thing they suggested farmers do to diversify—get into catfish—FmHA hung him out to dry. Attorney Phil Fraas noted in his later legal research that "the bloom is clearly off the rose." The agency's local office had used its authority as lien holder to sabotage Scott's prospects and starve his operation. This was to be the end of it.

Men with live haulers showed up and seined the ponds. The catfish were valuable assets, purchased and fed with some of the government seed money. Scott hadn't been expecting them. He watched from afar.

They're stealing my fish, he thought. Scott had no proof, but he assumed the men were with FmHA, a fact confirmed when he later inquired with the sheriff. The confiscation was contractually legal. The real theft had come more than a year before at that table with Delbert Edwards, when his own government treated Scott not as an equal but as a big, bad, troublemaking black farmer.

In the aftermath of the seizure, Scott shut off the irrigation and the ponds dried up. A few fish that had escaped the FmHA nets remained in the dwindling basin. It was the end of an era. Isaac trudged into the water in waders to make the final harvest. He was determined to process every fish left.

It had been a slow week at the plant, without enough work to keep everyone busy. Isaac pulled a johnboat through the water and tossed in fish from the shallows. Lillie Watson-Price took off her shoes and came in after Isaac to help. By the time Isaac noticed her, Lillie already had a fish in her hand. Isaac and Lillie poked around all afternoon. They scraped the bottom, grabbing the fish behind the head and hoisting them out. At the end of the day they had a few hundred pounds. They dragged their haul, with pruned hands, to the bank. Inside the plant, the workers processed them just as they would've done with twenty thousand pounds. When they were done, they headed home.

Scott and his workers embraced these tough times, eager to do anything they could to keep the business open. The prospect of hard, grueling work had always been a blessing compared to no work at all. They thrived in extreme conditions and thought of themselves as "catfish special forces." No job too dangerous or too odious. Lillie regaled the other Dependables with the episode. "We caught them by hand. . . . No boots, no nothing. Barefooted just like I came into the world."

Isaac walked by as Lillie punctuated her courageous tale with a dramatic pause. "Isaac, tell them," Lillie said to Isaac.

"And you were out there barefoot?" Eva asked.

"Because the mud was going to pull the boot off anyway," Lillie said with certainty. "And I thank God nothing stuck in my feet." She looked at Isaac. "What did you have on your feet?"

Isaac hid a smile. "Boots," he said.

They came for the farm equipment, too. Out of the blue one dark night, two deputies showed up to "attach" Scott's equipment, which meant locking up the vehicles so they couldn't be used. Attaching is often the warning shot, a sign that the land is next. Bank by bank, tract of family land by tract of family land, the foreclosures came. The only piece of Scott's land that the government had no claim to was his 160-acre homestead, bought from his father and brother, which included the ponds and plant that he'd dug and funded himself.

Isaac was home the night the deputies—one black, one white—showed up for the machines. He walked outside in jeans and a T-shirt to stop them. He told them to get off his dad's place. To leave the equipment alone. His eyes were still adjusting to the night when the white deputy pulled his gun and ordered Isaac back into the house.

Power structures in the South are inseparable from the legacy of white supremacy, which demands the establishment not just *be* in charge, but continually push down agitators who threaten the status quo. The officers were the instruments. It was their duty. But for the white cop it seemed personal, as it had from the outset with those at FmHA. It was as though he resented the changing times the Scotts represented.

Isaac turned around like he'd been told. The cop followed him toward the house, his pistol drawn. "He ain't bothering you. Let him go on to the house," the black deputy hollered after his partner. Isaac stopped and turned around to face the lawman with the gun. "You don't need to do this," the black deputy told the white one nervously. The white deputy put his gun away and took out a pair of handcuffs. He cuffed Isaac and shoved him in the car. Then both deputies went back and attached the last of the equipment. They took Isaac to jail and booked him for obstruction of justice. The sheriff, who knew the Scotts, heard the deputy reciting the charges and came in shaking his head. "Let that boy go home," he told the deputies. "He ain't doing nothing. You'd do the same thing for your daddy."

Scott did his best to farm rice and soybeans that year even as the foreclosures fell like dominos. He was cash-strapped and couldn't afford the diesel he needed to salvage what was left of his soybean crop; it, too, would go to pay down his outstanding loans. A white farmer nearby who was sympathetic to Scott's plight helped him keep his gas tank full. The farmer had more diesel than he needed; his own loan with FmHA covered as much fuel as he could ever hope to use.

In the middle of the night, Scott inched across a fallow field in his pickup with the lights off. He had three fifty-five-gallon drums in the truck bed. The stealth was to protect both himself and the reputation of the white farmer. Scott rolled to a stop in front of the pump, which the white farmer had left unlocked. He climbed into the back of the truck with the nozzle and pumped his drums until they sloshed full. He sat on the wheel well while he waited for the last one to fill. The smell of gasoline in the darkness reminded him of a still, early-hour pit stop on a long road trip. When he was finished, he put the nozzle back and crept away. He might do it again in a few days if he was running low. When Scott and the farmer passed each other in the hardware store, they didn't breathe a word about it. Is it stealing if nobody acknowledges that something's gone?

Isaac had land of his own. The banks came for that, too. When they foreclosed on Isaac, Scott was furious. He drove to his son's field with a can of kerosene and set fire to it like Sherman. The neighbors called him a firebug and joked that he was one day going to burn up the world. In Isaac's field, he tried. The blaze consumed everything but the dirt. Scott's face was hot. He watched from the edge of the field, silhouetted against the orange flames. In the aftermath, the authorities asked around but never brought charges. "I don't have a clue, now," a farmer next door told the police. "I didn't see nobody."

40 MINORITY CONTRACT

With his ponds empty, Scott was forced to change his business model to survive. As the foreclosures were under way, a catfish farmer called Scott unsolicited and asked if he could process a load of fish. Scott saw an opening. He conceded fish farming and rebranded himself a catfish processor and distributor.

Scott took advantage of opportunities that the big processors couldn't. Historically black colleges and universities such as Alcorn State University were loyal customers. He supplied Head Start, a flagship education, healthcare, and nutrition program of the U.S. Department of Health and Human Services. Thousands of young children grew up eating Scott's catfish through Head Start meal programs. He secured a profitable minority government contract as part of federal USDA commodity programs; he shipped fish regularly to Kansas City.

Delta Pride bid against Scott the next time the minority contract came up. According to Scott, they hired a black guy to set up a third-party company that enabled them to game the contract. This token middleman processed fish only on paper. FmHA, reiterated Scott, further meddled with the supply side by discouraging farmers to process fish with Scott. A man who sold catfish to Scott during these lean times had two heart attacks in less than six months and lost his farm after FmHA came calling for the money he owed. A farmer who broke the unspoken rules risked it all.

Growing up, Scott heard stories about how men crumbled and failed along with their yields. A farmer who lived near them, Edward Sr.'s best friend, "was working land on the west side of Brooks's plantation and looking how my daddy was raising cotton down there on the east side. Land that had never been farmed before. Just cleared out of the woods." Edward Sr. was making good crops, but his friend was failing.

One morning, the farmer was talking to his son out by the roadside. Standing in the highway for about an hour and a half telling him everything he was planning to do. "I've spent all the money on this land," the farmer said, "and I just can't grow cotton like that. I'm going to have to kill myself because I ain't going to make enough money to be here."

A few days later, the farmer's son was in the field working when he heard the loud report of a shotgun. He ran back toward the sound, saying over and over to himself, "Lord, my dad done killed himself."

He took his life because he owed so much on the land, Scott said. Only in death, through the grisly adage, could the farmer afford to buy the farm.

41 THE BRINK

The catfish boom was on. Scott had carved out a catfish portfolio of minority government contracts and key local clients. He bought from other farmers to fill these orders. Demand for Mississippi catfish was going up, but his supply dwindled. Scott believed that that FmHA and the industry were using their influence to blacklist him. With a pinch on supply, he scavenged for viable alternatives.

Industry-wide, farmers couldn't dig the ponds or raise the fish fast enough to keep up with demand. Around 1985, Church's Chicken put catfish on the menu to reinvigorate their southern franchises, signing on with six Delta distributors to buy eighteen million pounds of catfish over fifteen months.[1] A few years later, McDonald's launched its own experiment with catfish, developing a "crispy catfish sandwich" available at two hundred locations across Tennessee, Kentucky, Alabama, Arkansas, and Mississippi. McDonald's planned to serve the catfish patty with lettuce and tangy sauce on a home-style bun, the same bread used for the McRib sandwich.[2]

In the long run, both Church's and McDonald's cut catfish loose. But their willingness to put it on the menu was a sign of the times. Catfish had become mainstream. The wake from the steamrolling industry heavyweights pushed the little guys to the margins.

Scott rode into town to check his post office box on a warm Tuesday in April. He thumbed through the bills and grocery coupons and a day-late Sunday paper. He stopped on a letter from Gary, Indiana, and opened it as he walked out into the sunlight. It was from a catfish live hauler named Tommy Williams, president of Williams Fishing and Hauling.

Mr. Williams had a dilemma. The spike in demand from the Church's catfish experiment left some live haulers, like himself, without any fish to haul. "In the past two weeks I've had to turn down two separate people capable of taking 50,000 pounds of farm-raised catfish per month," Williams wrote.

Williams was black. He spoke to Scott openly, as if he felt an underdog blood tie from three states away. The fish shortage was hurting the black community, said Williams: the small businesses who served it and the minority distributors who sold it. "I am hoping," he wrote desperately, "somehow, you can expand your operation to help ease the fish shortage situation. We are going to need at least 750,000 pounds of fish per year . . . . We will be glad to do business with you and your operation."

Scott slid the letter back into the envelope. On the way home, he thought about what he'd write back. He wished he could tell Mr. Williams that Scott's Fresh Catfish would save the day. He wished he could say that his ponds were jumping. He wanted a partnership between the two catfish men and a black-owned network that stretched from coast to coast. But Scott knew his reply would be much shorter. Scott had touched the dream, only to watch it slip away. There wasn't much else for him to say.

42 EDNA'S KITCHEN

Scott's Fresh Catfish was an anomaly in the Delta, a landmark made historical in real time. To see the catfish plant in operation was to witness the genesis of the story, like hearing the blues of Sonny Boy or B.B. or Mississippi John Hurt before their names were known. Businessmen came to inspect the skinning lines and distribution system. Chapters of the Boys and Girls Clubs showed up to hear Ed Scott tell about what it took to eke prosperity from the earth. College professors and students visited. Writers navigated their way, drawn by hearsay, to walk on the concrete slab of the former tractor shed. They came to lay eyes on the only minority-owned catfish-processing plant in the nation. They stayed to eat at Edna Scott's kitchen and restaurant. She began it as a cafeteria for the workers, but it became an attraction on its own that fed plate lunches to bottomless bellies.

With miles of farmland in every direction, the only other way to get a hot lunch in the area would have been to raid a local domestic kitchen. Edna's oven and stove and pots and pans and recipes were not unlike those of other Delta homemakers. She made pies, beans, sweet potatoes, corn, and chicken using the methods and recipes passed down from the women who cooked before her. But like her husband, Edna had big ambitions. To accommodate the daily crowd, the Scotts built an annex to house Edna's restaurant. Inside were a kitchen and a dining room that could seat two dozen. At lunchtime, the dirt parking lot overflowed with cars. Customers waited outside for to-go orders and sipped sodas from the refrigerated Coke machine that the Scotts put at the corner of the house.

Edna started the day with breakfast for the workers. Her mise en place owned every available countertop. Eggs, onions, peppers, butter, slab bacon, biscuit dough. Edna owned the kitchen, but she didn't cook alone. She deputized the Dependables as sous chefs, and they helped with breakfast before they went to work at the plant. Edna's kitchen was as intimately hers as her dresser drawers, and the women felt privileged to share this space. They moved in the tight galley like dancers, weaving in front of and behind one another as they shifted skillets and opened the oven and pinched salt and seasoning.

Eva oversaw the bacon. The others had to act fast—Eva didn't let the strips cool for long before she ate them herself. The other workers screamed to her, "Save me some bacon!" from outside the kitchen window. By the time they got to the front of the line Eva could only laugh, mouth full. "Ain't no more! I done got it all myself."

Edna shared Christian devotionals and the love of Jesus along with the scripture of her recipes, which she wrote on little white cards. Her angel biscuits were famous. Lillie liked to say that knowing how to make those biscuits was how she got her first husband to marry her.

After breakfast, the Dependables walked thirty yards from the house to the plant. Edna, alone then, prepped for lunchtime. She planned her menu by what was around. In the family patch between the house and the cemetery she grew everything: okra, tomatoes, corn, squash, zucchini, butter beans, lima beans. "You name it, we grew it," said Daniel Scott. "We were pretty much self-contained out here."

Edna fried more fish in her kitchen than some roadside catfish houses. The workers never tired of it. They had a certain cognitive dissonance about the gore of the plant and the gourmet delights of Edna's restaurant. One minute they were covered in fish blood and feces. The next they sat under the trees and savored filets. When small fish, not sized for market, made it into the vats, Scott gave them away freely to his employees, who took them home in boxes like fat bonuses. The small fish, the Dependables said, taste the best of all.

Daniel described midday hunger on the farm as your "stomach hitting you in the back." The lunch rush brought the catfish workers from the plant and farmers from the surrounding fields. Edna had plates waiting for the men of the family, who ate voraciously. Though they didn't linger over lunch, they mapped their day by Edna's food; thinking about it all morning, savoring it for the rest of the afternoon.

Edna was as much a businesswoman in the home as her husband was in the field. She merchandised her famous fry mix of cornmeal and spices and called it Edna's Original. It was packaged in a folded-over white bag with black-and-white lettering. The workers swore it could make even off-flavor fish taste right.

43 DELTA TO D.C.

By the late 1980s Scott's business model was in jeopardy again. Though he was at full capacity with an army of employees, he didn't have enough work for them. But Scott was nothing if not resourceful. He'd been a catfish farmer and a processor. Now he became a fry master. Edna's kitchen and her famous cornmeal mix fed into this new endeavor. Like the process of deep-skinning that had set him apart from his competition in the early years, Edna's seasoned cornmeal elevated his cooked catfish.

Washington, D.C., twitched with energy in early January 1987. Mayor Marion Barry had been elected to a third term in a dominating performance. Later that month a snowstorm would cripple the city, but on this evening the weather was clear and warm. Three women stood on a street corner waiting to cross. Their eyes darted up and down the avenue. These were southern folk. This many cars, to their minds, usually meant a funeral procession or the after-service exodus from Mound Bayou First Baptist.

Elnora Mullins, tall and fearless with eyeglasses and gold teeth, stepped into the street as cars whirred past. The other two stood still on the curb. "Come on, y'all!" Elnora yelled from the other side.

The other women didn't budge. The constant flow of city traffic paralyzed them. They shook their heads firmly and held on to each other until the light finally changed.

These three Dependables had traveled with Scott to cook catfish at the inauguration party, as requested by Mayor Barry's people. Barry had roots in Mississippi. In Itta Bena, where Willena went to school. He wanted catfish as a celebratory accouterment. The Dependables had finished the prep and changed clothes a few hours ago. Now it was time to rejoin their employer at the harbor where the party boat was docked.

The mayor's camp told Scott to have dinner ready at six. The band was warming up on the boat when Scott dropped the first filet into his fryer on the dock. Sharp-suited, cocktail-dressed, and flashily accessorized guests walked past him to board.

About an hour in, Marion Barry and the revelers had worked up an appetite and came off the boat to eat. The mayor was dripping sweat. His face glistened. His top buttons were undone. He grabbed a piece of fish off the serving tray before Scott could even hand him his plate. He ate it fast and grabbed another. "Oh, god-dog I need some more of this fish," Barry said while he chewed. "It's good. It's good as I ever tasted."

Scott's most consistent catering clients were black politicians, who courted would-be voters at rallies and commemorated electoral victories with fish fries. Scott saw himself and his fried fish as integral to this acquisition of black political power. He identified with elected black officials who broke into white-dominated spheres. Washington, D.C., was the pinnacle of vested authority, and Scott—shirt tucked and apron neatly tied—felt like he owned the place.

44 CLASS ACTION

As Scott fought to stay afloat, he simultaneously worked to get his land back. There were programs in place, most notably one known as leaseback/buyback, under which farmers whose property sat in government inventory could work their land and, with healthy enough profits, hope to reacquire it. Bureaucracy tangled his efforts for nearly a decade. Scott requested a leaseback/buyback in 1986 and didn't get a real answer until 1995. FmHA told him later that his paperwork had somehow fallen "off the desk into the trash can or maybe it was under a stack of stuff." He filed complaints with USDA alleging discrimination by the local office; no response came. While this was going on locally, Congress and USDA moved to address countless claims of racial discrimination from across the country. In 1996 USDA initiated the Civil Rights Action Team (CRAT), tasked with investigating the agency's failures to service minority farmers.

"There are some who call USDA 'the last plantation,'" the CRAT report opened.[3] "An 'old line' department." Indeed, it was one of the last federal agencies to integrate and to appoint women and minorities to leadership roles. The agency was stubborn and slow to change. Many believed USDA actively allowed widespread discriminatory loan practices to fester. A 1990 proposed Senate bill sponsored by Senator Wyche Fowler (Ga.) of the Congressional Committee on Government Operations validated this notion; it directly accused FmHA—a minority farmer's "lender of last resort"—of accelerating the decline of black farm ownership in the country through unfair practices that did not consider the needs of the minority farmer.[4] The ambitious bill laid out policies intended to restore minority landownership to 1910 levels by the year 2000.

The 1990 bill didn't pass, and the tradition of African American farms remained in jeopardy. Scott's neighbor Howard Williams joked that "the black farmer in Mississippi needs to be on the endangered species list."

The CRAT investigation was followed by a lawsuit against USDA on behalf of a North Carolina corn and soybean farmer named Timothy Pigford. The suit named Dan Glickman, USDA secretary from 1995 to 2001, as the defendant. By August 1997 the case had grown into a class action suit on behalf of farmers across the country who felt they had been betrayed by USDA. Eventually, Scott became one of thousands of black farmers to join the lawsuit. It represented his last, best chance to get compensation for the loss of his land and livelihood.

Lawyers had been looking for a way to organize a successful class action suit against the agency. They needed "commonality"—something concrete to connect the experience of the Tennessee cotton farmer to the

Texas cattle rancher to the tobacco man from North Carolina. Phil Fraas, co-lead *Pigford* counsel along with attorney Alexander Pires, had the lightbulb moment reading a newspaper article in the *Richmond Times-Dispatch* in May 1997. He saw an article about how USDA had shut down its investigation of civil rights cases back in 1983.[5] The complaints were still coming in, but none were being addressed. *That's the hook*, Fraas thought. His class action would allege that there were two wrongs done. The black farmer didn't get the benefits the white farmer got, and when he complained about it, nothing happened. Fraas put down the newspaper and started scribbling notes. "That second aspect," he said, "is the same no matter where you are or what county supervisor you're dealing with."

45 D.C. TO THE DELTA

Attorney Phil Fraas is a thoughtful and deliberate man, a D.C. veteran who started in the U.S. Senate as counsel on the Committee on Agriculture, Nutrition, and Forestry beginning in 1975, and then on the House Committee on Agriculture from 1985 to 1989. Working both within and outside the federal bureaucracy has given him keen insights about the machinations of U.S. agriculture and an understanding for farmers' motivations and the challenges they face. Visiting the Delta and Ed Scott, he learned what grassroots discrimination looked like in practice.

"In Mississippi . . . FmHA was pumping just tons and tons of money . . . in the late '70s to keep farming afloat," said Fraas. "FmHA was probably loaning more money to farmers than even the commercial banks or the farm credit system. . . . Along with the local political head and the minister, the FmHA guy was right up there."

In rural communities the agency was a big deal, and its power went unchallenged. If the minister was the gatekeeper to the hereafter, the FmHA supervisor was the arbiter of farming salvation on earth. Oversight was relatively nonexistent. The state FmHA office was supposed to monitor the activities of the county supervisors, but the folks there remained on autopilot, managing the programs as they'd always done, vulnerable as ever to old-guard ambivalence. In Mississippi, "old guard" meant white. In the opinion of the U.S. Commission on Civil Rights in 1982, a society in which whites controlled virtually all elements of land production and development could never be equal. The imbalance reinforced the black community's long-held skepticism of American justice.

According to Fraas, when the *Pigford* case first started, the Justice Department people assumed they'd be rid of it quickly. Judge Paul Friedman, however, presiding over the case, firmly established that the decision would not be a formality. In the status conference hearing at the beginning of the trial, *Pigford* co-counsel Alexander Pires pushed to move directly into mediation. There was no defense for USDA ignoring the complaints from black farmers, Pires told Friedman. "If someone files a complaint and the government throws it in the trash—if that isn't a violation of your civil rights, I don't know what is," said Pires. The defense lawyer from the Justice Department pushed back against mediation and downplayed the legal grounds of the case, intimating that the class in which Fraas and Pires were grouping plaintiffs was illegitimate. Friedman didn't take the bait. He dismissed the lawyer's legal maneuvers. "[USDA] Secretary Glickman says in this morning's paper," Friedman told the defense, " . . . that he wants to resolve these cases. . . . That's what your client said on the Hill."[6]

In the referenced *Washington Post* article, Dan Glickman admitted the agency's fault in neglecting more than a thousand civil rights complaints and said, "Underneath the backlog, we're getting at the root problem."[7]

The defense lawyer (the only representative for USDA that day) tried to object, but Friedman continued. "Look, I think there is a class action here. I don't think we need any discovery on that issue. . . . I am prepared to certify the class and move forward, if you want to go to mediation. But I think you should go back and talk to your client."

Judge Friedman was sending a message to the USDA leadership and the Justice Department. If they thought his case was going away, they needed to adjust their expectations. This case was important, and Friedman would not allow it to stretch out in perpetuity, slowed down in the legal machinery just as the farmers' complaints had been.

"We got a sense early on that the judge was not going to treat this like a normal case of someone harassing . . . a government agency," Phil Fraas said. "That he was going to really try to figure out what the plaintiffs were . . . talking about. And I'm sure it's because he reads the paper, too. He could see the CRAT report and USDA basically admitting they had done wrong."

When many of these agricultural programs were developed in the 1930s, the Roosevelt administration cut a deal with the southern barons of the Senate. The senators promised Roosevelt their votes if he would allow them to run the farm programs as they wanted to. The wrongdoing had been simmering for decades. When Fraas showed up on behalf of Timothy Pigford and the other farmers, it all came to a head.

Clinton's secretary of agriculture and Glickman's predecessor, Mike Espy, had a lot to do with moving toward more agency transparency. Espy was the first African American secretary of USDA, part of a younger and energized group who saw a need for change. He was also from the Delta and knew firsthand the challenges of being black there. Espy helped start some of the conversations that eventually captured the attention of Congress and led to the CRAT report.

There were two camps within USDA. If the old guard's actions had been words, Fraas observed, they would be, "You don't screw with us, we control the money, we control the loans, and everybody's kissing our rear end." Then you had the reformers, who knew what had happened in the South and were looking for a path to a more equitable agency.

Soon after the class was certified, the plaintiffs got a break. Fraas and Pires had had a problem. There was a two-year statute of limitations for discrimination cases. So in 1997, Timothy Pigford and other farmers couldn't claim anything that had happened before 1995. Lawmakers and politicians, including Al Gore, pushed for an exception. In 1998 Congress would pass legislation that extended the statute of limitations back to 1981, two years before USDA disbanded its investigations of civil rights complaints and the same year that Scott was out digging his ponds on his own dime.

On April 14, 1999, Judge Paul Friedman—whom Phil Fraas calls the real hero in the case—issued a consent decree. He opened his opinion with a reference to forty acres and a mule, the promise of land and loans to former slaves after the Civil War. Freed slaves accepted the aid through the Freeman's Bureau. During Reconstruction, President Andrew Jackson reversed many of those policies, and the government seized and gave farmers' land to Confederate loyalists. The Department of Agriculture (established under Lincoln in 1862) began operations at this historical juncture. As USDA grew more influential in the twentieth century, the number of black farmers steadily declined. "Today, there are fewer than 18,000 African American farms in the United States," Friedman wrote in his opinion, compared with 925,000 in 1920. "The United States Department of Agriculture and the county commissioners to whom it has delegated so much power bear much of the responsibility for this dramatic decline." The agency's actions to delay and frustrate the loans of black farmers were "the culmination of a string of broken promises that had been made to African American farmers for well over a century."

The consent decree laid out the structure for compensation, but the plaintiffs and Ed Scott weren't to receive restitution just yet. The decision confirmed wrongdoing but not specific damages. To get damages, farmers had two options. Track A claims were handled relatively quickly; small farmers received payouts of fifty thousand dollars and forgiveness of remaining agency debts. Track B was for the larger operations like Scott's. Track B required a far more intensive process and a preponderance of evidence to get compensation commensurate to a larger farm. Only about 100 of more than 22,000 eligible farmers chose and successfully argued Track B cases.[8] Phil Fraas stayed on and worked with many of these farmers, including Ed Scott. To prepare the requisite file for Scott, he took a trip to the Mississippi Delta.

The longer Fraas spent in Mississippi, the clearer things became. Southern racism bloomed beneath the surface. "It's tough to put your finger on the wrongdoing from looking at these pieces of paper because . . . people covered themselves pretty well," Fraas said. But the longer he worked on the case, the more he began to see.

FmHA supervisor Delbert Edwards had retired and been replaced in the county office by a man named William Leflore. Fraas went to speak with him. He wondered if it was coincidence that Leflore shared a name with the county he represented. It had been named after Greenwood LeFlore, an influential Choctaw chief of Native American and French blood who fought for tribal rights against the infringing federal government during the 1830s and became an elected Mississippi state representative in the 1840s. Fraas asked the supervisor if it was so. "Yeah!" William Leflore said proudly. The chieftain had been something like his great-great-great-great-grandfather. That's how vested the power was.

Fraas looked with interest out the window of his rental car as he drove from the FmHA office to the Scott homestead. The land was beautifully austere but alive in ways Fraas didn't feel back in D.C. The absence of skyscrapers and pavement told him that man was subject to nature here. It was elemental earth. He felt like a settler in a new land.

Fraas couldn't remember the last time he was more than a hundred yards away from a paved surface. He nearly got lost trying to find Scott's home. Seldom a road sign. Just the recurring façades of white-painted churches that could be counted as mile markers. Fraas turned off the long, open highway outside Drew and entered the farmland on narrow roads that appeared out of nowhere. He drove for what felt like forever.

46 THE 22,000

For every large-scale black farmer like Ed Scott there were hundreds of smaller landowners who worked 40-, 80-, or 120-acre parcels. They too found themselves caught in the web of indebtedness and discriminatory government loan programs. Many of these farmers couldn't discern information about how the loan programs worked, what was available to them, and what rights they had.

Howard Williams owned the farm next to the Scotts. He qualified for the *Pigford* class action suit after he took an FmHA loan one year in the late 1980s. A drought hit hard that season and his crops suffered. He gave every penny he made to the banks and FmHA, but it wasn't enough. The agency refused him more money until he paid off the balance. Howard scraped together enough money to continue farming the next year, supplementing his income with his second job as a long-haul trucker. With his profits he incrementally paid off more of the loan. He never did hear anything from the county office. He just kept sending the checks and they kept getting cashed. This went on for three years until a man in a suit from the state FmHA office pulled into Howard's driveway one afternoon.

The man from the state held in his hand all of Howard's debt history. Howard was sure he was there to see about the rest of what he was owed. Howard told him he'd been working as hard as he could at two jobs to pay back that loan.

The man looked confused. "You should never be paying us any personal income," he told Howard. After all, FmHA didn't pay for the diesel in Howard's eighteen-wheeler or the bridge tolls on the cross-country highway. And they hadn't funded his farm in years. "Why don't you ask for a debt forgiveness?" the man asked.

Debt forgiveness? Howard didn't know what he was talking about. "If you can't pay," the man told him, "the agency is supposed to help you." *Well I'll be darned*, Howard thought. He asked the man, in jest, to forgive his debt right then so he didn't have to pay any more. The man nodded his head and began some paperwork. He drove away as the sun was setting and Howard never heard any more from FmHA about the money he owed.[9]

Howard was late to learn what his neighbors already knew. He went to the courthouse and looked in the public records, where he found that some of the nearby white farmers that he grew up with had been forgiven as much as $150,000. Meanwhile, the local agency office had allowed him to flail and wrestle with a crippling personal debt that was a pittance to FmHA.

Howard moved on from it. He knew he would never have an enterprise that spanned the generations. But he continued to farm because he loved it—ever since he was a boy and saw his grandfather in control on the tractor. "My granddaddy always taught me, don't worry about the other man and what he's doing, just do what you can do. . . . And that's still in me today. I don't give a darn what nobody else do. I just do what Howard can do."

Both Scott and Howard were hurt by the way FmHA treated them. These were men whose pride was tied to how hard they tried. They didn't take shortcuts. The tragedy was that their government hadn't allowed them to be their best farming selves. People knew about Scott's downfall; small farmers like Howard were simply forgotten.

47 NEEDLE

The fight had taken a toll on Scott. The plant was closed—Edna's cafeteria with it—and FmHA owned nearly everything. By the time FmHA granted Scott his option to lease the land in 1995, the government had designated 10 percent of the property protected wetlands, which made it even less useful. Scott was in ill health when the *Pigford* case began. He was done farming. His request to lease the land included a note from his doctor that outlined his ailments: prostate cancer, severe hypertension with cardiomyopathy, congestive heart failure, and advanced degenerative joint disease.

When the class action came along, Scott readied himself for a legal battle. He had no idea how protracted the process would be. Scott was seventy-six years old in 1999 when Judge Friedman ruled in favor of the black farmers. He was eighty-nine when Fraas finally argued his individual Track B case in 2011. He'd been diagnosed with a major depressive disorder and with late-onset Alzheimer's. He had lost one eye and was legally blind in the one he had left. He couldn't feed or bathe himself. The question was no longer whether Scott could bounce back in the farming business, but rather if he could hope to realize some semblance of justice within his lifetime.

When Phil Fraas took that trip to the Delta in spring 2007 to prepare for Scott's case, the processing plant was in disrepair. It became more decrepit with each successive visit, as if its health was somehow tied to Scott's. The fields and ditches around the home had grown wilder. Vines constricted the exposed posts and doorjambs. Scott had moved out of the house years before when his health first started to go and settled with Edna and their daughter Willena in Renova. The house by the ponds sat as empty as the grain bins.

Phil Fraas inherited all the files from Scott's previous lawyer. He sifted through big Tupperware tubs in Willena's living room. Willena had kept everything, but even she couldn't organize the files that came from the FmHA office—copied in duplicate and triplicate or upside down. Somewhere in what could have been 100,000 sheets and carbon copies, Fraas hoped, was the needle that could swing the case in Scott's favor.

FmHA's attitude toward the little guy proved to be one of Fraas's greatest assets. As much as bureaucrats avoided red-handed paper trails, their attitude of superiority toward black farmers could not be fully masked. They had been invincible for so long. Sitting in a sea of papers marked with agency seals, Fraas felt the government's powerful presence. He was trying this case against the biggest and baddest legal force on earth. Hundreds of lawyers with just one client: the United States.

From a pile beside him he picked up some correspondence between Scott's previous lawyer, Levi Boone, and the defense attorney for USDA. To substantiate the discrimination, Scott had to produce three white farmers approximately the same size as he who farmed approximately the same crops as he, and prove he had been treated differently. Boone had requested access to the personal financial records of three of Scott's neighbors, and USDA had agreed. In 2002 courts ruled that the government no longer had to make white farmers' files available. Farmers who hadn't known to ask were out of luck. But Fraas took the letter as a promise. With the documentation, he obtained the farmers' files. He had the beginnings of a case. After more long hours he found smoke. In FmHA memos that preceded the foreclosures, officials referred to Scott as a "big black farmer" who was out of his depth. Scott knew he'd been singled out for his skin color; the record agreed.

48 SCOTT AS STORY

Each year since 1998, the Southern Foodways Alliance (SFA) at the University of Mississippi has hosted a symposium. The program highlights chefs, cook, writers, and culinary personalities and shares diverse stories about southern food. For the inaugural symposium held in

Oxford, Mississippi, SFA director John T. Edge invited Ed Scott to cook catfish.

Scott was used to cooking for a different crowd. Gathered around him were university professors and scholars and a heavy percentage of well-to-do white faces. Not the same cross-section of the population he ran into at state fairs and blues festivals and "Save Mound Bayou" events and campaign fundraisers for members of the congressional black caucus. Scott set up on the open lawn outside the University of Mississippi Foundation. He wore his apron. The grease hit its bubbling stride.

Scott might have faded into obscurity when the plant closed in 1990 if not for writers like Richard Schweid and John T. Edge, who kept his story alive. They framed him not just as a farmer or a cook, but as a Delta titan whose name belonged in books.

"There's a way of telling a story in Mississippi that you don't run into most other places," said Schweid, who included Scott in his 1990 book, *Catfish and the Delta*. "Ed was an excellent raconteur and . . . a hard-headed Mississippi farmer. That's not a racial thing—that's much more of a Delta thing. . . . And the fact that he was black was just one more strike against him."[10]

At the symposium, Scott rolled filets in Edna's cornmeal mix. In a separate fryer he dropped dollops of sweet hushpuppy batter. He pulled the filets when they finished and let them drain and cool on paper towels. Folks came up to ask him about his technique; Scott told them he used vegetable oil because peanut oil was too heavy. They asked him about the time before; he told them about the fingerlings and the ponds and the struggle. He urged them to try a bite while they were standing there. And then the rhetorical question. *Ain't that the best fish you ever tasted?*

Scott was not an author in the same way that the academics at the symposium were authors. He wrote his epic in actions and feats. But over the years, Scott also sat at the typewriter to record what he had seen. One of Scott's most important documents is a three-page account of his plight in catfish that he presented in 1998 to a committee of President Clinton's One America in the 21st Century: The President's Initiative on Race. Scott served on a committee of six who informed the initiative's panel discussion about race and labor on the campus of Ole Miss. Scott's testimony was entered into the committee minutes and he was designated to represent the labor group on the public panel. "My son and I started our catfish operation with no money from FHA and we pulled ourselves up by our own 'boot straps,'" Scott wrote,

> ... with FmHA continuously refusing to lend us or any Black farmer enough money to adequately operate our farms. Of the more than 169,000 acres of land in Mississippi that are under water in catfish ponds, Blacks own less than 500 acres. This discrimination of lending practices made it impossible for me as a Black to secure funds to operate or expand my farming operation in row crops or catfish farming, processing, or marketing. This discrimination that ultimately led to my having to close my plant, has also affected the 85 employees and their families. Many of these workers remain unemployed even today, February 1998.

Scott took his eyes off the grease for a minute and the oil bubbled over, spilling onto the grass and bursting into flames. Some administrators hollered when they saw the pristine sod alight. Scott turned down his burner and watched the madness over the campus grass. The flames sucked the moisture out of the irrigated turf and left it singed and frizzed like hair. Scott thought about the time at the Delta Blues Festival when the boy helping him poured gasoline into the fryer instead of oil and nearly blew them all to pieces. That hadn't killed him and neither had anything else. The grass fizzled out. He turned his burner back up and waved some tentative onlookers over. He wasn't worried about this one. He welcomed the fire.

49 RECOGNITION

The Mississippi Delta is the epicenter of catfish farming. When it comes to cooking and serving the filets, the mecca might be the hamlet of Taylor in the Mississippi hill country outside Oxford. Here you'll find Taylor Grocery, owned and run by a man named Lynn Hewlett, whose fried catfish has won over generations of loyal patrons. The institution appears nearly derelict; a rusted fuel pump sits where it has since a boy with a neat part checked dipsticks and soaped windshields for nickels. The red brick is weathered white, and stray cats and dogs skitter across and beneath the porch. Taylor Grocery has used the humble catfish and the self-deprecating building to curate community on checkered table-cloths. The owners encourage guests to sign the walls in pen. Mississippi authors of world renown, municipal employees, grape juice Methodists, real wine Episcopalians, boisterous bourbon drinkers, sassy Shirley Temple sippers—all sign the walls. They're scrawled with thousands of names. If you've eaten there, you've become a part of the place, your mark tangible evidence of the culinary exchange.

In 2001, Taylor, a dogleg in the road, was the scene of a powerful and bizarre episode. John T. Edge and John Egerton, the founding corner-stone of SFA, had chosen the site for the Fourth Annual SFA Symposium. Attendees assembled in a nearby church a block away from Taylor Grocery to hear folklorists and lecturers talk of the transformative na-ture of food. Scott was invited for a special purpose. Not to cook his fish, as he had done for past SFA events, but as an honored guest.

"I couldn't help but admire a man with that kind of perseverance," said Hewlett. With the symposium and storytelling under way at the church, he was prepping for the posttalk catfish dinner, watching from the porch for the time when his guests would pour from the sanctuary. "[He was] going against the norm. . . . I don't know if that thing worked exactly like he envisioned it, but it did work."[11]

Scott had been summoned to Taylor to receive the SFA's prestigious Ruth Fertel Keeper of the Flame Award, named for Ruth Fertel, founder of Ruth's Chris Steak House. It was the first award the SFA ever bestowed.

In the church, Edge and Egerton called Scott to the front to accept his plaque. Scott stood and talked to the congregation about black entrepre-neurship, land, and the importance of holding on to a dream. Edge saw in Scott an embodiment of SFA's principles. "We care about using food as a way of exploring race and class. . . . The notion was, let's pay homage to Mr. Scott . . . and take this moment to let him step away from the fryer and up to the podium and tell [the] story and why it matters."[12] Scott's family was among the 150 in the sanctuary. Scott scanned the room until he found their comforting countenances. He thanked everyone and stepped away. His eyes were heavy with happy tears.

When the program concluded, the crowd walked the quarter mile over to Taylor Grocery for supper. As they walked along they heard strange music. Could it be? Bagpipes? A half-dozen kilted musicians stood roadside like they'd been dropped from a cloud. Folks were baffled. *Weird as hell*, Edge thought. "Daddy, did you know there'd be men in skirts?" said Willena. The group walked slowly past the hairy-legged pipers filling the air with exaltation. Lynn Hewlett waited at the end of the road. He looked pleased. It was going just as he'd planned.

The musicians had stopped by Taylor Grocery earlier in the day on the way to another gig. Hewlett asked them if they would stick around to surprise some friends of his, and they agreed. American bagpipe players from Tennessee performed ancient Celtic tunes in honor of the son of an Alabama sharecropper and Mississippi catfish mogul. They played to the crowd of symposium attendees from far and wide who had no idea across what otherworldly threshold they had passed, perhaps wondering whether some film crew had staged the whole thing and was catching their bewildered grins in the fading light.

The group, out of metropolitan Memphis, was called the Wolf River Pipers, Hewlett informed a buoyant Edge. Hewlett had told them to wait until the very moment that the church doors burst open.

At Taylor Grocery, Hewlett fed the Scotts. In that moment, the fried fish became something more. Hewlett felt the arc of time. He thought about the weight of what Scott had done in catfish and about how history is made by stubborn, tireless folk. His own place in the annals was mixed up with Scott's story like cornmeal and spice.

"Doing what he did where he did it, it was a big deal," Hewlett said. "*Is* a big deal. Not was. *Is*."

50 SETTLEMENT

Scott's farming life was thoroughly in the rear view by the time he accepted the SFA award. His court battle, though, was far from settled. *Pigford v. Glickman* moved rather quickly once it was affirmed as a class action in 1997, but it was more than a decade before Scott's claim was heard in November 2011. With evidence in hand, Phil Fraas prepared for Scott's day in court. One single day. Because of the volume of *Pigford* claims, the hearings were expedited and condensed into a span of a few hours. Fraas arrived to the D.C. conference room at ADR Associates, where arbitrator Michael Lewis waited with a group of staff, witnesses, and a reporter with a camera. The Scotts took seats next to Fraas.

Both sides had submitted direct testimony in writing, and each side had essentially four hours to cross-examine based on what had been submitted. Scott testified. Isaac testified. An economics expert and a few others testified. A doctor spoke again about Ed Scott's poor health and how his financial woes had hastened its decline. In addition to his witnesses, Fraas had the white farmers' files, which showed that Scott received disproportionately less in operating funds than his white neighbors and that his debts were scrutinized far more harshly. The pièce de résistance was the internal correspondence that Fraas and Willena found. Scott, the "big black farmer," sat pensively during the proceedings and didn't cause any trouble.

Though the claim was heard in one day's time, the case had been a war of attrition, and Fraas was exhausted. From the beginning, lawyers from the Department of Justice had thrown one motion after another to slow them down. The government lawyers were professional, but Fraas got the sense that just off-stage, some of the old-liners at USDA and the U.S. Office of General Counsel were furious about the whole *Pigford* ordeal. Some authority was being chipped away from the stone. That was the heart of the matter. From the D.C. bigwigs who let the system churn on to the pen strokes of Delbert Edwards, it had always been about power perverted and unbound.

A retired and aging Delbert Edwards was not deposed. A replacement from the Mississippi state FmHA office, a designated hitter, spoke for the agency. During cross-examination, Phil Fraas asked the man about the improvements Scott had made to his farmland that FmHA had cited as oversteps. Over the years, he had graded it to make rice drainage and irrigation more efficient. And there's the problem, the designated hitter said. Scott hadn't asked FmHA if he could grade the land.

"You mean [if] I've got a mortgage on my house," Fraas replied, " . . . but I put a new roof on, I've got to get it cleared with [my lenders] beforehand? I don't think I should. Because I'm just improving it, right?"

The designated hitter backpedaled. "No, no," he said, suggesting that maybe the agency didn't see the work as an improvement on the land. More likely, they had no interest in seeing Scott improve.

No further questions.

The attitude of the man from FmHA wasn't personal arrogance, Fraas recalled, but that of the agency itself. *You may be a black farmer running your operation with your own vision, but we're the ones who tell you what to do.* The arbitrator picked up on it, too.

On April 17, 2012, the arbitrator reached a final decision, concluding that FmHA officials had failed to adequately fund Scott's operations in the early '80s, withholding money with which he might have irrigated his crops and fed his catfish.

They had also failed to provide loan servicing to restructure his debts as they did with many white farmers. They refused to continue subordinating his loans to local banks in 1983, triggering a fire sale of his land. And they delayed his leaseback/buyback application for years while he struggled to regain his property.

Based on the value of those foreclosed 945 acres and real and projected lost earnings from 1981 to 2010 that ensued from his inability to farm, they awarded Scott millions. He was one of the final farmers to have his case heard in *Pigford*, and the ruling by the arbitrator signaled the close of the case. About 60 percent of the 22,000 plaintiffs prevailed in their claims for a total recompense of more than a billion dollars. Scott's land was gone forever, his empire dissolved, but he found some closure in the decision. It was the end of a long and drawn-out chapter.

51 A LITTLE DRIVE

Willena and Edna drive between West Cleveland and Ruleville in Willena's minivan on Highway 8. They are headed to the grocery store. Edna gave up driving long ago, but she likes to look out the window at the farms where she grew up.

These areas were once the domain of the black farmer. Ad hoc nations of their own. Thousands of the acres Edna sees out her window now aren't owned and worked by families anymore. Corporate caretakers watch over things from the sky by drone. There are hardly any houses dotting the horizon; far fewer independent farmers ride atop tractors. Intermittent signage marks the farms with a conglomerate's logo, some variation of a seed and a stalk and the shape of a sun and maybe a bird gliding. No way to know for sure what lies back in those huge swaths of private land. Used to be, everyman black farmers with names like Asa Zachary and Anderson Pound and the Morris brothers and the Williamses lived here. Now, who knows?

52 LAND GRAB

On a morning in 2012, Willena Scott-White read the local newspaper. She'd been retired for years now from her job as a public-school administrator, where she oversaw some of the same Delta schools that, decades after integration, were still struggling. The private academies that sprang up in the 1960s and '70s in response to integration widened the educational gap between the haves and the have-nots. As much as things had changed, they hadn't. Now Willena did contract consulting work and cared for her father, whose medical needs grew with each passing month. Her Renova home was a plainspoken ranch with clipped shrubs and a garaged minivan outfitted with special doors and ramps so she could wheel Scott in for his trips across the river to Little Rock for dialysis and treatment.

The homestead acreage in Leflore County, with its empty catfish ponds, vacant house, family cemetery, and caved-in processing plant, were all that was left of the parcel that FmHA couldn't take because it never held a lien. The grain silos Scott built for his rice still stood. An equipment shed sat in shadow, sheltering cobwebbed machinery from the sun. A small portion of the land where Scott's brother Alex once raised hogs was still arable. The Scotts leased it out to a nearby white farmer. Its presence only emphasized how little was left. When Scott received his compensation, he relinquished any claim he had on the seized land. The swaths in Leflore and the expanse in Bolivar had been sitting in government inventory ever since the foreclosures.

Willena flipped through the newsprint. She passed over the local sports section, the advertisements for two-for-ones and quick lubes and closeout sales and all-things-must-goes, and into the classifieds. One page was nothing but small text, outlining the annual land sales. Most were farms that had defaulted, owned by banks or the government. They would be bought up at a discount.

Willena had little interest in buying more land. But she read through the descriptions anyway. Her eyes settled on one entry. The seller, the paper read, was USDA. The entry didn't say much else, nothing about how the land had been used or who had lived on it, what gatherings might have been held there or the work that might have been done there. But Willena recognized it by the acreage. It was her father's land.

When foreclosed Mississippi farmland is up for sale, the previous owner has a three-year window to buy it back and settle any back taxes and penalties. If, in year one, a buyer makes the highest bid, that person must wait for that three-year period to come and go, without the prior owner stepping in, before he or she holds outright ownership. If the original owner decides to buy it back in year three, he or she would only need to compensate the new buyer the value of the land plus the property taxes the new owner may have been paying on it in those intervening years. If the third year comes and goes, the deed officially goes to the highest bidder.

One way former owners can stake their claim is to show up at the land sale and pay that year's taxes; if they don't show, the tracts go up for public auction in the afternoon. This was the second year that Ed Scott's land had been on the docket. It had passed by the family unseen in the obscure folds of the paper the year before. If Willena hadn't caught it in year two, the Scotts would have been in danger of losing their first right of refusal. Seeing it when she did gave the family time to put the money together and halt the runaway train.

Willena showed up to the sale with a cashier's check for the 2012 property taxes. The payment of roughly $20,000 would set them up to buy it back outright in 2013. Because there wasn't an active bidder, Willena would have to work with USDA and an appraiser to settle on the exact value for the property. The adjusted estimate would consider current land evaluations and the roughly 10 percent of the acreage that had been designated protected wetlands in the 1990s.

Willena walked out relieved. She'd thrown down a gauntlet, formal notice that the Scotts were coming for their property. USDA had hoped for a buyer. They just didn't expect it to be Ed Scott.

53 RESETTLEMENT

Just a few weeks before Christmas in 2013, Willena loaded her father and his wheelchair into the van. A blanket lay over his lap. Over the previous months, the appraiser had gone back and forth with the agency, and after a protracted negotiation they had settled on the price for 927 acres—about 600 in Bolivar County and the rest in Leflore.[13]

At 4:30 p.m. the day before, the agency office had contacted Willena and Phil Fraas. They asked if Scott would be present and if he would be signing for himself. If he was unable to sign, the office informed Willena, she'd need an extra level of approval before another could sign in his place. Willena hadn't seen her father write anything down in years, but she answered quickly. "Yes," Willena said. "He'll be able to sign."

The Scotts lived modestly. But Scott's condition—his cancer treatments, his dialysis, his medications—came with large expenses. His *Pigford* settlement was substantial, but there were very practical reasons why the Scotts might have decided against using it to buy back the land. They no longer farmed. To acquire the land would be to take on an enormous responsibility, and potentially a burden. Cash in hand after all his troubles would not have been a terrible way for Scott to end. But even as his eyes failed him, Scott never lost sight of the end goal. Every day leading up to the purchase, Scott asked Willena the same question. Do we have enough money to buy that land? Willena responded the same each time. "Yes, Daddy, quit worrying."

"They thought I would have given up before now," Scott said. "Either that, or that I'd spent all the money on cars or something and wouldn't have nothing to buy that land with. But they were mistaken.

"A woman told me once that I might shouldn't go to the bitter end. That the court may not give me nothing. 'Well they just won't give me nothing then,' I told her. 'I'm going to the bitter end.'"

The agency administrators who handled this final transaction were not the same people who had mistreated him all those years ago. But there was still tension when Scott rolled into the Greenwood office. He represented the blow to the agency's credibility that was *Pigford v. Glickman*. As Scott recalled, the lady officiating the exchange was skeptical that he'd be able to pen his name himself. Willena pushed her father's chair up to the table.

Scott had perfected his signature in Mr. Threadgill's rural schoolhouse. He'd signed a letter to Santa asking for a red wagon. He'd penned his name on the title of his first car and on a note to Edna. He'd scrawled "Scott" on his Army papers when he enlisted. He liked to pay cash, but when he used checks, he carved the letters with a flourish like Zorro. He'd signed leases and condolences and his last will and testament. One of the things he had learned in school was about John Hancock, the man who signed his way into history.

Scott held out his hand. Willena gave him the pen. He couldn't see the words on the page. Willena mentally urged his hand to the page. The staffer watched closely. She warned that no family member could help Scott sign. Scott put the ballpoint to paper. He remembered the reply letter he wrote to the live hauler Mr. Tommy Williams in 1985 telling him he was sorry he couldn't get him the catfish he needed. The pen sat relaxed in Scott's hand. Scott felt eyes on him. He moved his wrist. As it had on his and Edna's marriage license before he shipped off to war, his name appeared. It came out smooth. Like the ten-thousandth fastball off a journeyman pitcher's weathered fingers. "I can sign it with my eyes closed," Scott announced. He clenched the pin in his fist. "I couldn't see but I signed it," he said. "Wrote that thing real good too."

The land was theirs. Once they were home, Ed Scott cried and sang and prayed all evening long. He called Willena into the living room.

"Hold your head down here," he told her. "I just need to kiss you on the jaw. I'm so full I just don't know what to do. I just thank God. I thank you. I thank God. I thank you."

"Well, Daddy, I'm happy to do it. I'm glad God let you live with a sound mind so that you could know that this day has finally come."

54 THE OTHER SIDE

Reclaiming the land brought Scott's farming journey to a tight, neat close. But for the family, it was not the conclusion. The Scotts have plans. There is work to be done. They haven't farmed on any real scale in three decades. Their choice to farm again means rebuilding the infrastructure and mastering the craft once more. The goal is preservation of the land, and of a purpose, for generations to come.

Isaac Scott, his father's natural successor, will be instrumental. But he won't be able to do it alone. Daniel Scott represents the younger generation. He left the Delta after high school when he enlisted in the armed forces as his grandfather had done. In the Navy, he went to Mexico, Jamaica, Barbados, and the Far East. He lived in Seattle for a time and worked for Boeing. He saw places that his cousins never had. The more he traveled abroad to other people's homes, the more he thought about his own. The world held spectacular things. So did the Delta. "I don't have a problem coming back," he said. "Keep them from having to be burdened with it."

Those bold moments in the 1980s when Scott went for catfish glory are gone. Decay and death and rebirth have ensued. The perceived effects of time are most pronounced after long absence—the span between a young child's birthdays. The summer off between junior high and high school. A tour of duty in a far-off land. The beginning and end of a court case. The family hopes to salvage and restore what is left of the processing plant. No one will stand at stainless-steel tables and skin catfish again, but the family hopes to transform it into a historical site where Delta children will come to learn about what happened here and what it means. Willena pulled the worn HAND WASHING and EMPLOYEES ONLY signs from beneath the fallen insulation on the floor and set them aside for a possible exhibition space. The family's vintage photographs, they hope, will be on view, revealing Jheri curls and Lee jeans, new Chevrolets and old tractors, family dinners, Scott in an apron and hot grease at a state fair fish fry. Edna making clothes. Edna doing hair. Edna making dinner. Edna reading to her daughters. Men with seine nets, little boys who need more bricks in their britches working like men, thousands of wriggling fish in the vat, Isaac proud and happy in his straw hat.

Scott knew that there always comes a time when one generation gives way to the next. Edward Sr. had been fortunate to have him as a son to take ownership of the family name. Edna's father, Isaac Daniel, found in his son-in-law Ed Jr. a farming heir. Scott thought about them both when he got their land back. They looked down, pleased, when he signed the deed. God, Scott said, looked down. When the patriarchs passed and when his government turned on him, Scott kept the faith and felt the presence of a divine watchman. "You know in ninety-one years I had to have somebody standing with me and working with me," he said.

When Scott saved his father-in-law from ruin by buying the Mound Bayou farm for more than it was worth, Isaac Daniel swore he'd pay back the generosity. He repeated it on his deathbed. "Don't worry, Edward," Isaac Daniel said. "I'll be here with you to help you." But he died before he could, and Scott continued without him. Scott had been the provider and the rescuer, the figurehead and the father. It was time for him to step aside, too. All he had to do now was rest.

55 DREAMS

Ed Scott dreams. In his hospital bed beneath his daughter's roof, he waits out the afternoon in slumber. The lights are out and it's dark and cool. No one has cracked the front door to the outside heat for hours now. He is curled up, halfway between the fetal position and the crookedness that comes from sitting in a chair all day. Scott relives past years and past places in pastiche, like flipping through scrapbook pages or finding a fantasy location with a jab of the finger on a spinning globe.

In his dreams, he walks again. He speaks loudly and clearly with the tenor that defined him, no longer in the subdued tones of his last days. Scott, like anyone or anything old, was once young. When he closes his eyes, he moves capably and assuredly through those spaces once more.

It's Christmas Day. Scott is a boy. A celebratory energy envelops the farm and the fifty-one families who worked the land that year under the guidance of Edward Sr. The smokehouses and pantries are full. The air is crisp and fragrant. Scott stands in the yard. He watches his father pull out of the driveway, pickup truck overflowing, to deliver glad tidings and gifts to the neighbors.

Scott holds the handle to a little red wagon, brightly painted and new, that he awoke to find under the tree. Scott marveled that Santa Claus could fit the wagon through the chimney. It was probably a tight squeeze, which he decided was the reason Santa hadn't had enough room for the BB gun the boys had asked for. The wagon was more practical, more versatile. Scott is piling up sticks as high as they'll go in the Radio Flyer, trying for a big haul.

Another Christmas. Scott stands in front of the mirror shaving. Behind him, on the hook on the door, is a red robe. He nicks himself with the razor and a few drops of blood hit the basin. Against the white porcelain, the blood is iridescent. It spreads and dilutes until it appears as thin veils of cirrus.

When he is done shaving, he dons the red bathrobe and tightens the belt. He sits on the edge of the bathtub and puts on woolen socks. He reaches for his boots and laces them slowly. Standing, he catches himself in the mirror. He can hear voices in the living room. Children's voices. They, too, are waiting for Santa. Scott grabs his hat and the white store-bought beard and goes out to meet them.

He is a playfully devious inversion of the white, jovial Saint Nick. The young boys and girls on the farm have developed a healthy fear of this North Pole figure. He is their judge. Scott makes the rounds, going from house to house like his father did, spreading goodwill. At each door, he greets the neighbors and then he pulls on his beard as the mother and father, grinning, beckon their children.

When the children turn the corner and see Santa they scream and run for hiding spots. "Don't get me! Don't get me!" they wail, tearing through the house.

"I told them I was going to get them because they'd been bad. . . . I was going to get them and carry them off with me"—to the toy shop, one presumes.

As Scott dreams, Christmas approaches once more. The Delta days that stretched on in laborious infinity—from "can to can't," as the old folks say—have grown shorter. Though the house in Renova has lighted reindeer and candy canes in the yard and icicles hanging from the eaves, Scott doesn't look forward to the holiday with the same anticipation he did as a boy.

Christmas was just a few weeks away when Scott regained his property. The holiday is "just another day" for Scott now. "If the Lord lets me live, then thank the Lord. I'll live with peace and ease. I'm more peaceful now than I've been in a long time since I got the land deed. Got that land, slept real good that night. Woke up the next morning and hadn't even turned over in the bed. Peaceful.

"I dream about farming every night, all night," said Scott. The night before, he'd been pulling stumps from the earth and leveling the field. He planted corn. Rice. Soybeans.

On the dream farm, Scott maneuvered the tractor through his fields in smooth arcs. It was joyful, never-ending, eternal work.

"I dream about my daddy some nights. I dream about some of these old folk around here. When I'm dreaming about my daddy, they're happy dreams of him. When he died, I was a young farmer then. He didn't know how in the world I was going to farm that place. But I farmed every bit of it."

EPILOGUE

On October 8, 2015, at the age of ninety-three, Ed Scott died. The family held a home-going at First Baptist Church in Mound Bayou, Mississippi, and hundreds from all over the country gathered to pay their respects to the man whose reach touched, and continues to guide, so many. The family organized a program, with speeches and singing from nearly thirty folks, that went on for two hours. Through it all, Scott was present, not only in spirit but in the flesh. He lay at the front of the church, his casket open, an American flag draped across it in recognition of his World War II service. Mourners passed by to view his body. He was thin, a vessel emptied of its contents, and yet his face glowed through the rouge and powder. It would be overly sentimental to say he looked as if he was wryly smiling. But it is easy to imagine, in retrospect, that he might have been.

This was to be a joyous occasion, one sister proclaimed from the lectern, despite the solemnity of the loss. The Scott children had printed thick programs on glossy stock that contextualized their father's life. The cover depicted a wrought-iron gate laid atop a ghosted image of a grain field blanketed with a dense and ethereal mist. Those in the pews clamored for these keepsakes. Some waved fans bearing Scott's likeness. Even with the autumn breeze, the packed church was stuffy.

A long list of speakers and performers and storytellers followed. Each spoke and sang and moved with a deep Christian reverence. Representative Bennie Thompson, the congressional representative for the Delta district and a friend of the Scotts, said, "All of us here today have at least one story about Ed Scott. Most of us have two."

Deacon Roger Morris recounted his time serving with Scott on the church steering committee. When Scott came on board, it became the "do it" committee, the deacon explained. Scott had grown weary of the pace of progress—the "meetings about meetings"—and had taken control of the building improvement projects. Early one morning he called the deacon on the phone. "Meet me at the church," Scott told him. They'd discussed a new parking lot for months with no resolution. When the deacon arrived, still half asleep, Scott was in the churchyard with his backhoe tearing up the ground to make way for the pavement. The "do it" committee.

"I heard him say that many a day. 'Just go ahead and do it.' Brothers and sisters, it's all about work. We've got work to do. He said, *work while the day is light*. Night is on the way."

Do it! erupted the congregation.

"He reminded me of David from the Bible," said Pastor Earl Hall. "The Israelites were getting messed around with by a giant and along came the little guy named David to save the day."

Reverend Sammie Rash, a good thirty years younger than Scott, spoke next. He told about a time when he had vertigo and was bedridden. Scott showed up at his home to check on him. "I'm here to see the reverend," Scott told the man's wife when she answered the door. He walked to the back room where the reverend lay. "I hate to see you like this," Scott whispered, and he started to cry. Returning the next day, Scott brought with him a walker. "You're going to get up," he told the reverend. Using the walker, the reverend stood. Over the next week he used Scott's walker more and more, regaining some of his strength. The reverend was still weak and in recovery when Scott returned again. He was pleased to see the reverend upright. "You're looking good," Scott said, smiling. "Now give me back my walker."

During the eulogy, another preacher read from chapter 23 of the Book of Psalms. Shepherds. Green pastures. Shadows of death. Fear no evil.

The pallbearers carried the casket out into the sunlit afternoon and placed it in a horse-drawn carriage. A driver from Carriage Tours of Memphis patiently waited atop his perch as vehicles lined up to follow. He would lead the funeral procession through Mound Bayou, then the pallbearers would load Scott's casket into a hearse and drive to the remote family cemetery across from the ponds.

The buggy-led procession tied up traffic. Cars inched along behind it. Once Scott's body was in the hearse and the buggy pulled to the shoulder, traffic picked up speed. A roadside speed limit sign flashed nineteen, then twenty-two. 1922. The year Scott was born. Through Bolivar County, into Sunflower, and out the other side into Leflore, the caravan followed. The twenty-mile journey followed Highway 8 through the town of Ruleville and into the sparse, flat farmland. When they reached the turnoff to the farm, cars transitioned from blacktop to unmarked county road. Each kicked up a rolling dust cloud.

Forty-seven vehicles rumbled the two and half miles atop loose gravel—the most cars going this way at once in quite a while, perhaps since one of those rice festivals so long ago. Three turns—a right, a left, and another right—led the group past the five grain bins, the shaded equipment shed, and finally, to Scott's old home. The cars, when they stopped, blocked the road completely. Beneath the trees in the family cemetery, mourners gathered. The immediate family stood under a tent near the freshly dug plot; others paced around the gravestones of Edward Sr. and Juanita and Laighton and Alex and others.

More than a hundred people had closed in around the tent by the time the final ceremony began. A web of brothers and sisters and cousins and nieces and nephews and in-laws from half a dozen states. The roster was innumerable. Many had been at the church for the service, but others were just now joining the ranks. Farmer Howard Williams pulled up in his pickup and walked over to pay his respects. He still wore the clothes and baseball cap he'd had on in the field. Howard had been working. Ed Scott would have understood.

Three black veterans from the Mound Bayou VFW stood in full regalia behind the pastor. Two younger soldiers in uniform accompanied them on either side, one with a bugle. As the veterans struck a rigid salute, the bugler played "Taps," the wailing notes that accompany a military funeral, and also, at dusk, signal "lights out." Time to sleep. Daniel Scott had hoped there'd be a twenty-one-gun salute, if only to hear the reports echo over the fields again like they did when he was a boy and the farmers chased the blackbirds off the rice crop with shotguns.

A pallbearer turned a crank and seeded Scott's body into the ground. A gust of wind picked up from across the fields and rattled the buckles of the tent against the poles, metal hitting metal, ringing softly.

When it was done, cars turned around in the dirt road to leave. There was no room to back out the way they'd come. The only exit was through an adjacent soybean field, empty and withered. The vehicles filed out through the dirt, over the dried remnant soybean stalks, which folded over and sounded off beneath the tires.

THANKS

Willie Morris was, when he wasn't burning oil at his writing desk, an amateur magician. He pulled a dollar out of my ear in 1990 at our neighbor's home-turned-restaurant-and-bar in Shaw, Mississippi. In this manner, many children found many dollars in the otological shadows, and all heard Willie tell them the same: "There's a gold mine in your ears." For those who find their callings in fiction, his is a statement about the multiverse of imagination. For those like myself, fueled by esoteric truth, his wisdom suggests listening—to sagas spoken in soft tones by ancient orators.

My father, Tom Rankin, and mother, Ruthie Ervin, encouraged my curiosity and instilled in me purpose and a passion for making. My formative years in Oxford, Mississippi, during its early and mid-'90s golden years introduced me to storytelling as a thing normal men and women did, and one that a society might celebrate as surely as it did SEC football. I did not, then, know how writing was done, but I knew how writers and cultural advocates ought to live and act, thanks to the examples of Richard and Lisa Howorth, William and Marcie Ferris, my godparents Charles Reagan Wilson and Marie Antoon, Larry Brown, Jonathan Miles, Jim Dees, Ron Shapiro, Jimmy Phillips, and many others.

My English and creative writing professors at the University of North Carolina at Chapel Hill, including Laurence Naumoff, Minrose Gwin, Daphne Athas, Daniel Wallace, and Randall Kenan, gave me my first taste of craft. Their lessons and friendship have been indispensable. Thanks to the countless writers who have influenced me through the years, including Allan Gurganus and Tim Tyson, who showed me what it means both to practice and to preach; and to Jill McCorkle for her ongoing support and advice.

Without the trust and hospitality of Willena Scott-White, the daughter of Ed Scott Jr., this project would never have begun. She advocated for this telling, invited me into the family home, educated me, and shared with me the most personal and sensitive resources from the family archive. She introduced me to a multitude of kin and friends, who in turn lent to me their time, patience, and stories. My sincere gratitude to them all: Edward Logan Scott Jr., Edna Ruth Scott, Willena Scott-White, Isaac Daniel Scott Sr., Rose Marie Scott-Pegues, Edward Logan Scott III, Vivian Scott-Chatmon, A. D. Chatmon, Octavia Scott-Pack, Joseph White III, Isaac Daniel Scott Jr., Felisha Claudette White-Edington, Eva Brooks, Lillie Watson-Price, Essie Watson-Maggitt, Elnora Mullins, Carrie Curry-Cooper, Dollie Scott-Mosley, Howard Williams, Greg Carr, Ben Morris, John Morris, Harvey Green, and others.

I am likewise indebted to those who spoke with me as my research expanded: authors John T. Edge and Richard Schweid, whose prior work about Ed Scott paved the way; Charles McLaurin, a veteran of the movement who gave me firsthand accounts of the life and work of Fannie Lou Hamer and her compatriots; Ron and Sylvia Myers, who shared their catfish activism over taco salads in a Belzoni, Mississippi, Mexican joint; Helen Sims of the Reverend George Lee Museums in Belzoni; Jennifer Rose and the staff of the Sunflower County Library in Indianola; Lynn Hewlett of Taylor Grocery; and attorney Phillip Fraas, who guided me through the history of Ed Scott's legal battle in the landmark *Pigford v. Glickman* case.

From our first meeting in his Oxford backyard in 2013, John T. Edge encouraged me and shepherded the development of this narrative. In his role as director of the Southern Foodways Alliance, he and his staff made possible a writing retreat at Rivendell Writer's Colony in the mountains outside Sewanee and the publication of an early excerpt of this book in sfa's *Gravy Quarterly*. As a mentor, he gave far more of his time and self than I could have asked for. His eyes, editorial guidance, and fast-twitch pen helped mold this project from bloated draft to finished product. As series editor of the University of Georgia Press's Southern Foodways Alliance Studies in Culture, People, and Place series, he helped create a platform for this story.

Brett Anderson, on the series advisory board, gave the manuscript an early close reading and offered welcome critique, as did Todd Moye and Richard Schweid. Thanks also to Elizabeth Engelhardt and Psyche Williams-Forson of the series advisory board for their support and trust. And perhaps no one has spent more time with the various iterations of the manuscript over the years than Sarah Camp Arnold Milam, SFA Managing Editor, whose professionalism and talents have been integral.

The University of Georgia Press made this book a reality. To Lisa Bayer and the press's staff and leadership I am extremely grateful, with special thanks to Acquisitions Editor Patrick Allen, who helped put (and keep) the process of publication in motion, and Production Manager Melissa Bugbee Buchanan, who pulled many of the pieces together. Thanks also to Mindy Conner, whose copyediting has no doubt eased the reader's journey.

Without the patience and support of my wife, Caroline Croom, I would not have made it nearly this far. To thank her is to also recognize her one-of-a-kind parents, Edward and Kay Croom. My only brother, Alexander, will surely see my faith in and love for him reflected in this book's characters; he is proof that role models are not always our elders. Thanks to Malcolm White for his ongoing belief and example, which help me sojourn on.

I don't have adequate words to thank Edward Logan Scott Jr., this book's hero and mine, who carried himself with grace until the end, and whose incarnate determination gave me the inspiration to pursue my first book through difficulty and false starts. Though the Delta is flat, the man climbed mountains. I hope he'll live forever in these pages.

NOTES

PART I. SEED

1. Ed Scott Jr., Community Oral History Project, filmed by Pat Farr (University of Texas El Paso, 1989), partially funded by the Mississippi Humanities Council; archived in Sunflower County History Room and Archives, Sunflower County Library System, Indianola, Miss.

2. Ed Scott Jr., interviewed June 28, 2013, by Julian Rankin.

3. Ed Scott Jr., interviewed April 14, 2013, by Julian Rankin.

4. Scott family lineage, compiled by Willena Scott-White.

5. Ed Scott Jr., interviewed July 13, 2013, by Julian Rankin.

6. John Hope Franklin, lecture at President Clinton's Initiative on Race, Oxford, Miss., March 11, 1998, William Winter Institute for Racial Reconciliation, https://vimeo.com/28058305.

7. Rose Marie Scott-Pegues, interviewed October 12, 2013, by Julian Rankin.

8. Ed Scott Jr., interviewed June 1, 2013, by Julian Rankin.

9. Brenton G. Wallace, *Patton and His Third Army* (Harrisburg, Pa.: Military Service Publishing, 1946).

10. Maj. Gen. Robert M. G. Littlejohn, "The Food Situation in the European Theatre of Operations," *Quartermaster Review* (January–February 1944), Army Quartermaster Foundation Inc., http://old.qmfound.com/food_wwII.htm (retrieved July 15, 2017).

11. "Handling Fast Freight on the Santa Fe," *Railroad Gazette* 39, no. 8 (August 25, 1905): 184 (retrieved July 15, 2017).

12. "The Red Ball Express, 1944," U.S. Army Transportation Museum, http://www.transchool.lee.army.mil/museum/transportation%20museum /redballintro.htm (retrieved July 15, 2017).

13. Story of James Chappelle, in "Personal Stories: Red Ball Express," U.S. Army Transportation Museum, http://www.transchool.lee.army.mil/museum /transportation%20museum/personalstories.htm (retrieved July 15, 2017).

14. Trezzvant W. Anderson, *Come out Fighting: The Epic Tale of the 761st Tank Battalion* (Salzburger Druckerei und verlag, 1945).

15. James Baldwin, *The Fire Next Time* (New York: Vintage International, 1993).

16. "Davis Bend, Mississippi (1865–1887)," BlackPast.org, http://www.blackpast.org/aah/davis-bend-mississippi-1865-1887 (retrieved July 15, 2017).

17. "The Jewel of the Delta: Mound Bayou, Mississippi," Preservation in Mississippi, https://misspreservation.com/2011/07/12/the-jewel-of-the-delta-mound-bayou-mississippi/ (retrieved July 15, 2017).

18. "Howard, T. R. M. (1908–1976)," BlackPast.org, http://www.blackpast.org/aah/howard-t-r-m-1908-1976 (retrieved July 15, 2017).

19. "UA Professor's Biography of T. R. M. Howard Returns Civil Rights Leader to Prominence in American History," University of Alabama News Center, Uanews.ua.edu, http://uanews.ua.edu/2009/08/ua-professors-biography-of-t-r-m-howard-returns-civil-rights-leader-to-prominence-in-american-history/ (retrieved July 15, 2017).

20. Willena Scott-White, interviewed June 8, 2013, by Julian Rankin.

21. Isaac Daniel Scott Sr., interviewed June 8, 2013, by Julian Rankin.

PART II. STALK

1. "Civil Rights 101: School Desegregation and Equal Educational Opportunity," CivilRights.org, http://archives.civilrights.org/resources/civilrights101/desegregation.html (retrieved July 15, 2017).

2. Baldwin, *The Fire Next Time*.

3. Edna Scott, interviewed June 29, 2013, by Julian Rankin.

4. "Selma to Montgomery (1965)," Martin Luther King, Jr. and the Global Freedom Struggle (King Encyclopedia), http://kingencyclopedia.stanford.edu/encyclopedia/encyclopedia/enc_selma_to_montgomery_march/ (retrieved July 15, 2017).

5. Olivia B. Waxman, "James Meredith on What Today's Activism Is Missing," Time.com, June 6, 2016, http://time.com/4356404/james-meredith-50th-anniversary-march-against-fear/(retrieved February 21, 2018).

6. Harvey Green, interviewed August 13, 2013, by Julian Rankin.

7. Kay Mills, "Fannie Lou Hamer: Civil Rights Activist," Mississippi History Now, http://mshistorynow.mdah.state.ms.us/articles/51/fannie-lou-hamer-civil-rights-activist (retrieved July 15, 2017).

8. Charles McLaurin, interviewed August 24, 2013, by Julian Rankin.

9. Peter Dreier, "'I Question America': Fannie Lou Hamer and the Battle for Full Citizenship," Huffington Post, http://www.huffingtonpost.com/peter -dreier/is-this-america-rememberi_b_5715135.html (retrieved July 15, 2017).

10. History of Freedom Farm document, circa 1977, authored by unknown Hamer associate; obtained from Charles McLaurin, 2013.

11. "About Dr. Todd," The David B. Todd, Jr. Foundation, http://www .dbtoddjrfoundation.org/about-dr-todd/ (retrieved October 18, 2017).

12. Jimmy Ellis, "Nashville Then: 1968 Civil Rights Movement in Nashville," *The Tennessean*, http://www.tennessean.com/picture-gallery/news/2014 /02/24/nashville-then-1968-civil-rights-movement-in-nashville/5775413/ (retrieved October 18, 2017).

13. Obituary, Charles D. Bannerman, 45; rural development expert, *New York Times*, April 19, 1986, http://www.nytimes.com/1986/04/19/obituaries/charles -d-bannerman-45-rural-development-expert.html (retrieved October 19, 2017).

14. Stephen A. King, *I'm Feeling the Blues Right Now: Blues Tourism in the Mississippi Delta* (Jackson: University Press of Mississippi, 2011), pp. 111–112.

15. Ben Morris, interviewed June 22, 2013, by Julian Rankin.

16. "History of USDA's Farm Service Agency," U.S. Department of Agriculture, https://www.fsa.usda.gov/about-fsa/history-and-mission/agency-history/index (retrieved July 15, 2017).

17. Charles Dodson and Steven Koenig, "Evaluating the Relative Cost Effectiveness of the Farm Service Agency's Farm Loan Programs," report of the Economic Policy Analysis Staff, Farm Service Agency (August 2006).

18. Kenneth Clayton, "Southern Agriculture in an Era of Expanding Exports," *Southern Journal of Agricultural Economics* 14, no. 1 (1982): 31.

19. Vera J. Banks, *Black Farmers and Their Farms*, U.S. Department of Agriculture, Rural Development Research Report no. 59 (July 1986).

20. Animesh Ghoshal, "The Effect of the Embargo on Grain Exports to the Soviet Union on the Exchange Rate," *Nebraska Journal of Economics and Business* 20, no. 3 (1981): 37–46, http://www.jstor.org/stable/40472697.

21. T. L. Wellborn Jr., "The Catfish Story: Farmers, State Services Create New Industry," USDA *Yearbook of Agriculture* (1983): 298–305.

22. "The Catfish Capital of the World: Humphreys County, Mississippi," City of Belzoni, Mississippi, http://www.belzonims.com/cfcapital.htm (retrieved July 15, 2017).

23. Martin W. Brunson and Donald F. Mott, "A Historical Perspective of Catfish Production in the Southeast in Relation to Avian Predation," *Proceedings of the Seventh Eastern Wildlife Damage Management Conference* (1995): 23.

24. Martine van der Ploeg and Craig Tucker, *Managing Off-Flavor Problems in Pond-Raised Catfish*, Southern Regional Aquaculture Center Publication no. 192 (August 1999).

25. Willard Scott, quoted on *The Today Show* in 1985, Simmons Catfish, http://simmonscatfish.com/about_us.html (retrieved July 15, 2017).

26. Phillip Fraas, interviewed July 13, 2013, by Julian Rankin.

27. Daniel Scott, interviewed July 1, 2013, by Julian Rankin.

28. Ed Scott deposition for Track B claim, circa the 2000s.

29. Eva Brooks, Lillie Watson-Price, Essie Watson-Maggitt, and Elnora Mullins, interviewed July 20, 2013, by Julian Rankin.

30. Candice Ellis, "Pickets in the Land of Catfish: The African American Labor Rights Struggle in the Catfish Industry of the Mississippi Delta, 1965–1990" (master's thesis, University of Florida, Gainesville, 2012), http://ufdc.ufl.edu/UFE0044281/00001 (retrieved July 15, 2017).

31. Charles McLaurin, interviewed August 24, 2013, by Julian Rankin.

32. Glenn Mosenthin, "Mississippi Boasts First Black-Owned Catfish Processing Plant in U.S.," Mississippi Department of Agriculture and Commerce, March 3, 1983.

33. John T. Edge, "Delta Pride," *Saveur* 53 (September–October 2001): 28.

34. Letter to Ed Scott from Jim Buck Ross, Mississippi Department of Agriculture and Commerce commissioner, February 28, 1983.

PART III. REAP

1. Mike McCall, "Church's Chicken May Be Key to State's Catfish Industry," *Clarion-Ledger*, January 27, 1985, H.

2. Associated Press, "McDonald's Tries to Hook Customers with Catfish Sandwich," February 13, 1991, http://www.apnewsarchive.com/1991/McDonald-s-Tries-to-Hook-Customers-with-Catfish-Sandwich/id-8bbab1421b9f1f087afa58743803a980 (retrieved July 15, 2017).

3. Civil Rights Action Team, "Civil Rights at the United States Department of Agriculture," Washington, D.C. (February 1997).

4. S.2881, U.S. 101st Congress (1989–1990), https://www.congress.gov/bill/101st-congress/senate-bill/2881/text (retrieved July 15, 2017).

5. Pamela Stallsmith, "Ignored since '83, Complaints Will Need New Investigations," *Richmond Times-Dispatch*, May 25, 1997.

6. Transcript of U.S. District Court, Status Conference Hearing before the Hon. Paul L. Friedman, October 24, 1997.

7. "Agriculture Dept. Lags on Blacks' Complaints," *Washington Post*, October 24, 1997, https://www.washingtonpost.com/archive/politics/1997/10/24/agriculture-dept-lags-on-blacks-complaints/1ddfb4bb-ea14-465f-9d94-7fcdd627f656/ (retrieved July 15, 2017).

8. Tadlock Cowan and Jody Feder, "The *Pigford* Cases: USDA Settlement of Discrimination Suits by Black Farmers," Congressional Research Service, May 29, 2013.

9. Howard Williams, interviewed June 22, 2013, by Julian Rankin.

10. Richard Schweid, interviewed July 27, 2013, by Julian Rankin.

11. Lynn Hewlett, interviewed January 20, 2014, by Julian Rankin.

12. John T. Edge, interviewed July 6, 2013, by Julian Rankin.

13. Willena Scott-White and Ed Scott Jr., interviewed December 7, 2013, by Julian Rankin.

BIBLIOGRAPHIC COMMENTARY

In conceiving this book, I treated the oral histories of Ed Scott and other family members as primary text. In addition to their prodigious memories, the Scotts kept detailed archives of photographs, legal documents, artifacts, personal correspondence, newspaper and magazine clippings, genealogical histories, and financial documents. This foundation of fact grounds the history contained in this book; the recollections of Ed Scott flesh out that environment and give it life. This is Ed Scott's story, told by him and seen through his eyes. Likewise, interviews with more than a dozen others, who gave generously and honestly of their time, are part of this book's DNA.

After a series of interviews conducted in spring and summer of 2013, I pored over the notes of Willena Scott-White and lawyer Phil Fraas, and public documents pertaining to the *Pigford v. Glickman* case, which provided a definitive legal architecture of Scott's life. Fraas's notes from the 2000s, which are part of the family's archive, tracked Scott's modern farming life and interactions with lenders year by year beginning in 1971. These facts, figures, and public records supported Scott's own telling of his life. And yet Scott went much further, back to childhood and to war and to stories that he had seldom if ever shared and that had never been written down. The bulk of the narrative comes from interviews I conducted, but another integral primary source was a video recording of Ed Scott housed at the Sunflower County Library in Indianola, Mississippi. This video was the result of a community oral history project conducted in the area by Patt Farr from the University of Texas at El Paso in 1989. Without this recording of Ed Scott giving a tour of the processing plant and conversing in his office, I would not have been able to see with such vividness the catfish plant—and Scott—in motion.

Many years before I knew of Scott, other writers interpreted his story. Among them is Richard Schweid, whose book *Catfish and the Delta* (Berkeley: Ten Speed Press, 1992) is an education about the human landscape of the Delta catfish economy in the 1980s and '90s. Locals talked to Schweid as if Ed Scott were Bigfoot. Schweid tracked him down and gave Scott's story prominence on the page. John T. Edge, director of the Southern Foodways Alliance, further illuminated Scott's accomplishments when he framed him as a heroic figure in a 2001 *Saveur* magazine piece.

Many of the historical moments and eras that Ed Scott lived through have been previously chronicled. Without such scholarship I could not have immersed myself in the circumstances of his times that was crucial in preserving Scott's authentic voice. In this book, these histories—such as World War II and the civil rights movement—are contextualized through Scott's experience and firsthand accounts. Readers will find other, more definitive and comprehensive histories about many of these topics, including: *Black Maverick: T. R. M. Howard's Fight for Civil Rights and Economic Power* (New Black Studies Series) by David T. Beito and Linda Royster Beito (Champaign: University of Illinois Press, 2009); *The Senator and the Sharecropper: The Freedom Struggles of James O. Eastland and Fannie Lou Hamer by Chris Myers Asch* (Chapel Hill: University of North Carolina Press, 2011); *This Little Light of Mine: The Life of Fannie Lou Hamer (Civil Rights and Struggle)* by Kay Mills (New York: Penguin, 1994); *Silver Rights* by Constance Curry (Chapel Hill, N.C.: Algonquin Books, 1995); *Selma, 1965: The March That Changed the South by Charles Fager* (Boston: Beacon Press, 1974); *The Patton Papers: 1940–1945* edited by Martin Blumenson (New York: Da Capo Press, 1972); and *Dispossession: Discrimination against African American Farmers in the Age of Civil Rights by Pete Daniel* (Chapel Hill: University of North Carolina Press, 2013). Certainly this book is inextricably linked to and influenced by much of the seminal writing about southern life over the last century, among them *A Childhood: The Biography of a Place*, by Harry Crews (New York: Harper & Row, 1978) and the masterwork, *Coming of Age in Mississippi*, by Anne Moody (New York: Random House, 1968), both of which I first read as a boy.

Southern Foodways Alliance
Studies in Culture, People, and Place

The Larder: Food Studies Methods from the American South
edited by John T. Edge, Elizabeth Engelhardt, and Ted Ownby

Hog Meat and Hoecake: Food Supply in the Old South, 1840–1860
by Sam Bowers Hilliard

To Live and Dine in Dixie: The Evolution of
Urban Food Culture in the Jim Crow South
by Angela Jill Cooley

Still Hungry in America
text by Robert Coles; photographs by Al Clayton;
introduction by Edward M. Kennedy; with a new foreword
by Thomas J. Ward Jr.

Catfish Dream: Ed Scott's Fight for His Family Farm
and Racial Justice in the Mississippi Delta
by Julian Rankin

Creole Italian: Sicilian Immigrants and the Shaping of
New Orleans Food Culture
by Justin A. Nystrom